amped

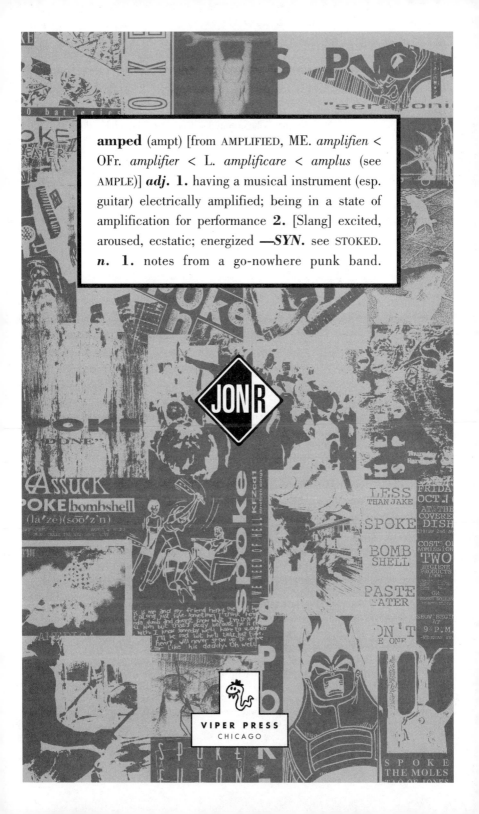

amped (ampt) [from AMPLIFIED, ME. *amplifien* < OFr. *amplifier* < L. *amplificare* < *amplus* (see AMPLE)] *adj.* **1.** having a musical instrument (esp. guitar) electrically amplified; being in a state of amplification for performance **2.** [Slang] excited, aroused, ecstatic; energized —*SYN.* see STOKED. *n.* **1.** notes from a go-nowhere punk band.

VIPER PRESS
CHICAGO

Amped: Notes from a Go-Nowhere Punk Band

Published in the United States by
VIPER PRESS
P.O. Box 3394
Chicago, Illinois 60690-3394
info@viperpress.com
www.viperpress.com

First Printing

ISBN: 0-9677908-0-8

Library of Congress Cataloging-in-Publication Data still pending as of this printing.

The "Spokehouse" chapter appeared previously on www.SixSpace.com.

"Sound System" lyrics by Operation Ivy from the album *Energy*, used with permission, courtesy of Lookout Records. "Persistent Vision" lyrics by Rites of Spring from the album *End on End*, used with permission, courtesy of Dischord Records. "The Busy Girl Buys Beauty" lyrics by Billy Bragg from the album *Back to Basics*, used with permission, courtesy of BMG Music Publishing Ltd., all rights reserved. Image on the the "Spoke" chapter banner by Charles Burns from *Skin Deep*, used with permission, courtesy of Fantagraphic Books, Inc. Excerpt from *Points of Rebellion* by William O. Douglas, 1970, Vintage Books, New York, p. 32.

Printed on 50% recycled paper with soybean inks by McNaughton & Gunn, Saline, Michigan.

For this printing, a donation has been made to **The National Tree Trust** (1120 G Street NW, Suite 770, Washington DC 20005, 202.628.8733, www.nationaltreetrust.org), which has planted more than 7.2 million trees in America's rural communities and urban areas, as well as provided tree maintenance and education programs nationwide; and **The Nature Conservancy** (4245 N. Fairfax Drive, Arlington VA 22203-1606, 703.841.5300, www.tnc.org), an organization which preserves habitats and species by purchasing land globally, having presently acquired more than 70 million protected acres around the world.

Cover and book design by

Photos (back cover, opening page and dedication page) by Kevin Rose

Special thanks to Linda Saracino, Vince Resh, Patrick Hughes and Dave Frank for the monster edits and continuous encouragement. And thanks to Rob Ray for the use of his truck and for being a rad guy.

Recorded material by Spoke available at www.NoIdeaRecords.com.

1

5

10

15

20

28

30

35

37

40

42

52

54

57

59

61

71

76

78

81

86

92

95

102

106

109

151

153

154

159

TO CHUCK AND SCOTT
AND EVERYONE WHO STUCK AROUND
FOR MORE THAN TWO SONGS

> *My music is best understood by children and animals.*
>
> IGOR STRAVINSKY

start here

Music is essentially useless, as life is.

GEORGE SANTAYANA

Get this guitar away from me.

I can't stop playing it. I'm hunched over it three, four, sometimes five hours a day. I've postponed work, sleep, eating, *everything*, just to play a few more chords. Pathetic.

Rather than take responsibility myself, I'm blaming Satan. Considering that the electric guitar has long been branded an "instrument of the devil," I figure I'm just another helpless sap who's fallen under the same spell as Buddy Holly, Chuck Berry, Gene Vincent and anyone else who's traded a place in heaven for three chords and a fuzzbox.

My current instrument of the devil is a Fender Stratocaster. Its body was free of damage until last night, when I knocked over a strange religious icon I bought at the Waldo Flea Market, near Gainesville, Florida — my home from 1988 to 1994. The icon, a wood plank holding a small crucifix with painted orange flowers, bears the words "Legend of the Dogwood." On the back, among mysterious burn marks, is written:

At the time of the Crucifixion, the dogwood was a large tree and its timber was used for the cross. Today, the tree is bent and twisted, never again to be used as a cross. It blossoms in the form of a cross — in the center of the outer edge of each petal there are nail prints brown with rust and stained red, and in the center of the flower is a Crown of Thorns, so that all who see it will remember.

The icon fell and took a dime-sized chunk from the side of my Strat, a minor dent. Perhaps this "accident" was Christ's attempt to save me from my unholy musical obsession, to purge myself of the Satanic guitar. It hasn't worked.

All of this began around 1986 when I was 15. I was fiddling with the Goya acoustic my mom used to play in her '60s cafe days. She never complained about what I was doing to her poor Goya, playing it in a way no acoustic guitar was ever meant to be played, pounding the strings viciously at appropriate hardcore speeds. Eventually, fed up with its folky tone — my Angelic Upstarts and Stiff Little Fingers renditions sounded like the Kingston Trio in a torture chamber — I bought a used $80 yellow Lotus Strat copy for my birthday, which I wound up keeping for the next four years.

I had only one lesson in my life, given by an old skateboarding buddy named Jeff. I used to watch in awe as Jeff blazed through Motorhead, Circle Jerks and Hüsker Dü songs with profound grace and ease. He taught me the basic power chord: any note played on a guitar can be intensified and enriched by making a simple three-finger chord out of it. From this uncomplicated technique, I learned the mechanics of the scales, their similarities and differences, how they fit together to form different chords, and which scales are most naturally linked to build melody structures into songs. Even today, as I experiment with amelodic riffs and off-scale progressions, I still love hammering out power chords most.

I played my Lotus for two years with no amplification, which is like eating Twinkies with a head cold — weak sustenance and no flavor, save a faint sweet aftertaste. My tinny strummings had all of the audio muscle of a toy ukulele, so I had to imagine powering the Lotus through an overdriven Gaellin-Kruger to keep my inspiration high.

I bought my first amplifier — a little Roland, about a foot tall — while living in the college dorms in Gainesville. I played it through a pair of headphones full blast to get maximum distortion without deafening my roommates. The piercing, distorted din was really amazing, like a chainsaw revved so high the chain was about to fly loose and dismember anyone within a 10-yard radius. And it could be heard through the headphones up to 15 feet away — it was *that* loud. Needless to say, I fried pair after pair of cheap headphones, not to mention ears.

About a year and a half later, with a handful of songs completed, I beckoned two close friends from high school, Scott Huegel and Chuck Horne, to move to Gainesville and start a band. They did.

More on them later.

Better equipment was needed, so I saved enough money to buy a used Ibanez Roadstar guitar from an ex-girlfriend named Cindy, a cool goth chick who wore eye shadow exquisitely. I adored her and promised to put "THANKS CINDY" in big block letters on the back of the guitar if she sold it to me, and to this day the back of that old Ibanez (or what's left of it) reads "THANKS CINDY." In the end she never checked out our band, not even to see her name on the guitar, and buying it was one of the last times I saw her.

I spray-painted the body of the Ibanez into a thick swirl of fire-engine red, bright chartreuse and royal blue acrylic. Over the course of a few hundred practices and shows, the colors were dulled by sweat and spotted with dried maroon bloodstains, my cuticles having been occasionally shredded from bashing away at the thin metal strings. While touring, I'd use the Ibanez and its case to prop up my head like a pillow. At home, I'd fall asleep in my underwear playing my guitar, awakening the next morning with it laying on my chest, my ribs aching like hell.

From this instrument, a band was begun. We called ourselves Spoke. We threw together some songs, played some shows, put out a 7-inch record and went on small tours. We then played more shows, released more records and eventually recorded enough songs to be collected onto two albums.

During that time, I wrote almost 50 songs on this guitar — in my bedroom, in others' bedrooms, in a moving car, on my porch, on a curb somewhere a thousand miles from home. I leapt, fell, leaned, whirled and flailed on-stage, and was picked up by others into the crowd off-stage, with my guitar strapped on and plugged in.

Then, with our "peak" yet approaching, we ended our band — because we wanted to, because the time was right.

I didn't choose to write about the three of us making music because we did it well. Not so. We weren't very good at all. But the music we played was music we put every ounce of ourselves into, music that pulled us to our emotional core, music that made us feel *alive*. Our sole aim was to express ourselves as clearly and intensely as possible, to bring the simple melodies playing in our heads to life. Those who liked the same kind of music, who saw the world similarly, who felt what we felt — they joined in. We all had a fuck of a time.

Many people who deserve to be recognized in this volume are not. To them I apologize. What made our band electrifying was the incredible support and participation of those who involved themselves with us, from releasing our records to simply showing up and rocking out at our shows. (In the great punk tradition of ludicrously extended thank-you lists, a roster of folks who gave us a hand appears at the back of the book.)

All of the accounts described in the following pages are true — or are, at the very least, as I remember them. Scott and Chuck may claim that some sequences occurred differently, but in the selective filter that is memory, this is how I experienced them. To the greatest degree achievable, the facts are in order, but we're all limited to our own narrow perspectives, and this is mine.

Many bands have better stories to tell than ours — bands who went a lot farther, longer and crazier than Spoke, bands who had greater musical skill, artistic depth and wild abandon than we ever did. One day I hope to read their stories too.

And, most importantly, I should mention that our experience is by no means unique. Kids around the world are continuously whipping up wild-ass noise for the sheer adventure of playing music, as they have for decades. Their songs may not be heard and their stories are rarely told, but they're still doing it. New bands are emerging even as you read this, wreaking sonic bedlam and spitting fire.

Which brings me to why I've bothered writing this, as you're probably questioning the merit of writing about punk rock instead of just leaving it the fuck alone. Well, at the risk of sounding maudlin and over-the-hill, I figure it's a good story for my grandkids, assuming one day I have some. I want them to know that the drooling, sodden geezer they see mumbling to himself in the rocking chair was once ablaze with passion, having the time of his life singing about any subject he could mold into a song, thinking nothing of the ass he was making of himself. I want them to know that, if they're inclined, they should do the same, or pursue whatever passes for "fun" and "art" in their day, regardless of how stupid it may seem at the outset.

In the meantime, though Spoke is long gone and the state of underground rock'n'roll has drastically changed, I still have my Stratocaster, and playing it ignites me as much now as the first time I ever gripped a full E chord, for which my gratitude is beyond words. Without a guitar I would've had no outlet to quell the clamor in my head, no medium to release the fire in my blood, and no reason to be on a stage in the first place, for which I got into so much awesome, hilarious, unforgettable shit.

And, as always, I can't stop playing it.

I'm too amped.

CHICAGO
DECEMBER 2000

spoke

Hell is filled with musical amateurs.

GEORGE BERNARD SHAW

"Shit. Sorry."

Our first show.

"We, uh... We..."

We murdered our third song on the opening note.

I had started too fast. Trying to compensate, Chuck pounded a beat we'd never heard before. Scott was just lost.

"Let's try that again," I said.

We could sense that the crowd of friends kind enough to attend our debut performance were suddenly embarrassed for us, like we were standing before them naked. The room was silent — a nervous, hard kind of silence, which was exactly what we were dreading because we knew this kind of silence *hurt*.

"Ready, Chuck? Scott?"

Chuck clicked his drumsticks together three times and delivered an assertive downbeat on the snare, as if to say *get this right, dipshits*.

We did. At that moment, it seemed my sole responsibility as a human being was to hold those chords like a vise grip — which, given the state of my nerves, wasn't easy.

If I had anything to be thankful for, it was that we weren't upstaged by the venue, Club Gravity. The building housed similar clubs in the years before, few of which passed fire code, most of which possessed an ambience rivaling the interior of a septic tank. My only real memory of its former incarnations was seeing a show there my first week of college when it was called (if I'm not mistaken) Club Moonshine. I remember sawdust sprinkled on the floor (leading me to wonder if it was a butcher shop by day), and when I entered the men's room I found a guy leaning on the sink getting a blowjob, the sawdust grinding into the knees of the woman servicing him. That nobody in the bathroom seemed to think this was unusual — that's what impressed me.

Playing on the same stage three years later, trying my damnedest to keep up with Chuck and Scott, I couldn't help but wonder if anybody was getting a blowjob in that bathroom now — a considerable improvement to watching us, I thought.

"*Ow!* What the fuck was that?"

Scott backed away from the $19.95 Radio Shack microphone, rubbing his mouth with his hand. He was announcing the next song when he got a sharp kiss of raw voltage on the lips: the mike wasn't grounded. It was connected to a bottom-of-the-barrel P.A. system (it picked up the radio frequency of nearby taxi drivers), which sat atop a rickety plywood stage. This stage was so unsteady that even the mildest of rock'n'roll acrobatics would surely cause it to collapse sideways, sending the over-enthusiastic performer flying through the storefront's plate-glass window.

Club Gravity's possession of a liquor license was questionable, but that didn't stop the manager from selling Pabst Blue Ribbon from a cooler. Ceiling beams, floor tiles and fuse boxes were left in disrepair; paper refuse, beer cans and piles of dirt were spread all over. The air, hot, dank and still, reeked of the stale, sweetly rotten aroma of dried beer — the unmistakable odor of downscale clubs worldwide, one I would forever associate with playing live. Hence the ideal setting for our public debut: sweat, garbage and stench.

That we even got the gig was luck. The headlining band, The Youngies, needed someone to open for them. They were nice guys and good musicians, playing a kind of Beatles/Bowie/Clash mishmash, occasionally destroying their equipment while covering "I Wanna Be Your Dog" for a finale. Our warehouse space was next to theirs, so they invited us onto the bill.

Actually, it wasn't even our warehouse space. It belonged to some friends in a great local band called The Jeffersons who vacated the room — roughly half the size of a one-car garage, maybe smaller — for better space elsewhere. The electricity was left connected and the door was never locked, so The Jeffersons passed it on to us — graffiti, broken glass, smashed electrical sockets, roaches, holes in the wall and all. Free practice space is mighty hard to pass up.

Every night we'd pack our gear into Scott's car and make the 15-minute trek. Frogs, mosquitoes and odors of mysterious origin welcomed us each evening. So did the unrelenting roar of novice speed-metal bands in adjacent warehouse rooms. To our left was a band called Golgatha, named after the mountain on which Christ was purportedly crucified. To our right was a band called Anathema, which, according to my dictionary, means "a thing or person accursed or damned." We'd never get them straight — they were equally horrible — so we referred to them both as (*in guttural Satanic voice:*) GOLGATHEMA.

Because they actually paid rent and were granted the privilege of locks on their doors, the members of Golgathema could leave their big equipment at the warehouse safely. As bigger equipment usually means louder noise, we heard their songs better than our own. My "starter" amplifier — a puny 30-watt Crate weakling (I soon sold it) — was no match for a mighty Marshall stack on the other side of a three-inch sheet of plaster masquerading as a wall. Sometimes practicing really sucked.

Out of necessity we became friends with the metalheads, having grown weary of their nightly habit of intentionally out-voluming us and trashing our space after we left (a new fluorescent light in the ceiling lamp, for instance, would always lay in shards on the ground the next day, forcing us to practice in the dark and step on broken glass all night). Because most of them were no different from the garden-variety headbangers we'd gotten into trouble with in high school — stoned round-the-clock, smart as a gerbil and generally as harmless — we got along okay.

This didn't make their music any better — Anthrax and Sepultura covers, no matter how polished, are never good — nor did it make the graffiti they scrawled all over the parking lot any easier to look at; AIDS KILLS FAGS DEAD and RAP SUX DIK are dismal even by metalhead standards. We eventually added to the warehouse's deterioration as much as anyone — kicking holes in the walls, scribbling our own graffiti (YANNI RULZ) — until the cops were called enough times that the owners kicked everyone out, erecting a barbed-wire fence around the complex and vowing never to rent to "musicians" again.

But that was long after our first show. Until then, we dedicated every spare moment to practicing, reserved for the late evening hours since no other time was compatible with our respective schedules. I was working at a local pizza shit-hole in the afternoons, the paltry check providing for rent, utilities and guitar strings. Luckily, just in time for the fall semester, I was fired for being (in my asshole boss' words) "defiant."

I guess he wasn't without reason. At the time, I was embarking on these all-night flier crusades to promote local shows — frantically designing layouts, scamming photocopies at Target Copy Center, staying out until sunrise plastering the town. By the time I'd get to work at 9 a.m., I was about as productive as a sack of shit (though exactly how this constitutes "defiance" still eludes me).

Fliers were a passion for me, and certainly more important than making crappy pizzas. I loved the challenge in creating a graphic that would stand out among the sea of advertisements stapled to telephone poles and public bulletin boards around town. One major fliering obstacle specific to Gainesville (for a while, at least) was this lunatic vagrant who wandered the city indiscriminately tearing down whole walls of fliers. At first I thought this was maybe his personal environmental mission, since the ecologically dubious act of fliering is barely a rung above littering. After careful observation, I realized no, the guy was just nuts. (Rumor has it a Gainesville councilwoman was so impressed with his anti-flier zeal, she put him on the city payroll.)

The first flier for our band was a poster-sized photo of two dogs having sex, taken by Henri Cartier-Bresson on a rainy cobblestone street in the '30s. Announcing our first three dates, the flier included a show at the Hardback Cafe — the club we would later call home — where, within an hour after we put the flier up, it was removed.

"It's got nothing to do with censorship," said Alan, the Hardback's owner, after I delivered a knee-jerk tirade about how he was infringing on our First-Amendment rights. "It's grossing out customers during lunch. They say they can't eat while looking at a couple of dogs fucking."

Still, the flier proved effective. More people showed up at Club Gravity than expected, spoiling us to the reality of ill-attended future gigs where, in more instances than I care to remember, we'd play to rooms devoid of any living presence save ourselves and the flies hovering around us.

Having burned through every song on our set list, I was relieved to see we had only one number left, a sort of Misfits-meets-New Order collision called "Care." By now, everyone in the audience was heckling us; this was good. Heckling is customary in Gainesville to express appreciation for a band's performance. If you ever play Gainesville and locals shout *pussies go home,* it means your performance is highly esteemed.

As we opened "Care," the sound emanated richly through the room. Our instrumentation was tight, and finally the music was progressing smoothly. I started to relax; the burden of hitting the right notes in time or singing the right words in key was lifting. I could just play and observe and savor the closing moments of our first show.

Everything looked weird from the stage. The audience seemed to flatten into a blurred, kinetic wallpaper of barely luminescent, indistinct faces behind an orange veil of cigarette smoke and stage light. The microphone, centered below my eyes, seemed to protrude from my mouth rather than extend to it. The sweat running off my left elbow made a slow, steady stream down my wrist and settled at my fingers, soaking the fretboard of the Ibanez, making the strings slick and easy to play, making them shimmer and gleam.

As we cracked open the crescendo that ended "Care" — a wave of four chords ascending at full-throttle — the raw, hard sound soaked deeply into my bones. With the drums, bass and guitar locked in rhythm and fused in melody, the noise seemed to unify into a dense force that shook the room — bringing to life something hot with sound, movement and emotion, something greater than the three of us individually, something that took control.

That's when it began.

Spoke was playing us.

scott

A great flame follows a small spark.

DANTE ALIGHIERI

When I met Scott Huegel, he was blowing up cars.

We were 15. Like me, he had moved from regions north to Longwood, Fla., among the dullest of Orlando's cookie-cutter suburbs. He skateboarded and drew skulls on his Converse Chuck Taylors, and spent lots of time listening to copied 7 Seconds tapes and re-shaving his mohawk with an old pair of dog clippers. So from the start, we had plenty in common.

I talked to Scott for the first time one morning in the Lake Brantley High School cafeteria. Many acquaintances — girls, mainly — told me not to hang around him, claiming he was a pathological liar, a troublemaker. But he seemed okay to me, maybe a little misunderstood.

A week later he was in jail.

Scott wasn't a criminal, nor were the neighborhood kids he hung out with in the spiritless subdivision of Wekiva Cove. But together at night, with stolen beer and nothing to do, they destroyed things. Cars, mailboxes, screen doors, lawn furniture — I don't know the exact inventory of targets, but all were items readily accessible to anybody wandering the vacuous Wekiva Cove streets looking to fuck shit up.

Scott was arrested and sent to the county's juvenile detention center for a few months, where he managed to resist fights from fellow inmates and overseers. He was released with something like 8,000 hours of community service, assigned the life-enriching task of cleaning police-station toilets.

When he returned to school, he might as well have had "ex-con" branded on his forehead. Everybody was suspicious (teachers and administrators included), speaking in whispers behind him. Rumors flew as to whether he was raped in the detention center (he wasn't), whether he was beaten senseless by a Latino gang (he wasn't), whether he was dealing drugs (he wasn't), or whether he was "changed" — meaning, I guess, repentant. He wasn't.

By court order, he couldn't meet with his Wekiva Cove friends, who had their own legal problems to worry about. What he needed was a pal, someone with whom he could goof around without getting into too much trouble. He called me.

From then until graduation, Scott became my main ally in combatting the near-constant state of after-school boredom that permeated Longwood; in him, I found someone who was as easily amused as I was. We devised many activities to keep ourselves from shrivelling in languor, most involving the huge, indestructible 1976 Chevy Caprice he drove, which we called the "Li'l Hog."

There was "Trash Day," which was Thursday afternoon. We'd drive around the peaceful suburban streets crashing the Li'l Hog into trash cans on carefully manicured front lawns one after another, leaving smashed containers and garbage strewn in our wake.

When it wasn't Thursday, there was "Poochie," in which a maniacal neighborhood dog (Poochie) would chase the Li'l Hog, nipping at its tires. We'd blare Raunch Hands songs and scream like wild idiot rednecks at bewildered neighbors as we fish-tailed all over Poochie's dirt road.

Or "Quaalude Day," where Scott would pull the Li'l Hog in front of a stream of cars and slow traffic to 10 miles an hour as we pretended to function in slow motion ("quaalude"). Sometimes it would result in full-blown traffic jams behind us, the drivers leaning on their horns and wishing us an early grave in the worst language they could think of.

When we weren't finding new ways to entertain ourselves, we passed the time bitching about the abysmal state of the world. Entrenched in the apathetic, selfish climate of the Reagan era, there was much to despise for two young insurgents in suburban, materialistic, right-wing America. We spewed the kind of rebel rhetoric that feels good to say but doesn't get much accomplished — "Passivity Equals Compliance," "Fight to Unite," etc. — most of which we learned from punk songs. Living in an almost all-white community, our militant anti-racism went even more against the grain, if not with the marginally bigoted local citizenry than with the large infestation of neo-Nazi skinheads, who were constantly giving us shit.

And it was with Scott that I spent a lot of time skateboarding, crashing parties and chasing girls. Scott — blond, brash and rugged — was good at attracting the ladies. I, however, looking like Darby Crash playing *Leave It To Beaver*, didn't have it so easy. Lacking in the charming-wiles department, I had to resort to being a nice guy, which usually got me dumped.

As I'm an only child, Scott grew to be the closest thing I'd ever have to a brother — which meant, at the time, a 24-hour pain in the ass. We bickered all the time. His natural disposition — concurrently sarcastic and sincere — got under my skin like a splinter; his best attributes — his intelligence, spontaneity, integrity, wit — soured on me. The only thing missing was the same set of parents and a bunk bed.

Upon graduation, Scott attended community college in Orlando. It was when he decided to join me at the university in Gainesville that we talked seriously about starting a band.

In Fall 1990, while I was in New York taking a semester off to work, I phoned him to discuss our yet-to-be-formed group.

"Hey, what do you think of the name 'Spoke?'"

The line was silent. I thought he hated it so much he hung up.

"Scott?"

"Spoke," he repeated. "That's pretty cool."

"Yeah," I said, relieved. "It's short and intense and easy to say."

"Where'd you come up with it?"

"I don't know. Popped in my head, I guess. The past tense of 'to speak.'"

"Right."

"I think it works."

"But," he said, "there is an Embrace song called 'Spoke.'"

"Shit. That's right."

"Is that where you got it from?"

"Well, no, not directly. I mean, subconsciously, who knows..."

"People will think we got it from them."

"Maybe."

"Or they're gonna think of it as a bicycle spoke."

"Wow. I didn't even consider that. I was thinking grammatically."

"Yeah."

"But that doesn't bother me too much."

"Me neither."

"People will butcher it, though. Think of it: Spook, Spork, Spock..."

"...Spooge, Smoke..."

"...Speck, Spackle, Stroke..."

"It'll be brutal."

"Yeah."

"So you have some songs written?"

"Uh-huh," I said. "A bunch."

"What do they sound like?"

"I think I played a few for you over the summer."

"I don't remember."

"It's... well, just stuff in my head."

"Like what?"

"I don't know. Fugazi-sounding, at times. Some Hüsker thrown in. Lots of Naked Raygun, obviously. Maybe Sonic Youth, early Joy Division. I'm afraid it'll end up sounding too much like Superchunk or something..."

"Well, that wouldn't be so bad. So you wrote just the guitar?"

"No, vocals too."

"Really?" He snickered. "I've never actually heard you *sing*, Jon..."

"Well, shit. I'll try. Hey, have you been playing your bass much?"

"Every day."

"What about Chuck? Is he into drumming?"

"Yup."

"He'd be willing to move to Gainesville?"

"Hell yeah. He's not doing anything in Orlando but picking his ass."

"You think he'll go for 'Spoke'?"

"I'm sure he'll be cool with anything."

"Hey," I said, "how do you think this stuff will go down in Gainesville? You think anybody would dig a band that wasn't doing the same old bullshit?"

"We'll find out."

The "same old bullshit" meant any of the lame genres that Gainesville's then-stagnant music scene was mired in — pre-grunge wank rock, post-R.E.M. frat-friendly pop, various shades of patchouli-infused hippie music — all falling under the idiotic banner of "progressive" music, later dubbed "alternative." Bored with the status quo and inspired by the few good bands in the area — Stabilizer, The Jeffersons, Strongbox and, above all, Naomi's Hair — we decided to give it a try ourselves.

1991 was a cool year to start a band. Musically, exciting things were happening everywhere. Fugazi was continuing to redefine punk aesthetically and philosophically in Washington, D.C. Big, hybrid rock sounds had been emerging full-force from Seattle through a then-cultish record label called Sub Pop. College towns like Chapel Hill, Olympia and Austin were homes to some of the most challenging and creative pop scenes in the country, taking the spotlight away from over-hyped rock meccas like New York and Los

Angeles. Touch & Go Records in Chicago was continuing to release the most innovative, visionary rock'n'roll in the world, while independent labels, small distributors and college radio stations throughout the U.S. and Europe had developed over the decade into a well-networked entity. A confrontational, highly political female consciousness was gaining momentum in punk scenes everywhere under the umbrella categorization of Riot Grrrl. And the burgeoning Gilman Street scene in Berkeley, Calif., had exploded with the likes of Operation Ivy, Samiam, Mr. T Experience, Crimpshrine and Green Day, among many others. Fueled by all of this energy, it seemed like a crime *not* to start a band.

Our musical ability, however, never matched our passion to make music. In Scott's case, the bass guitar was by no means his life-long calling, though he did play with more consistency and heart than most "accomplished" bassists around town. To him, the bass was something new to learn and enjoy, an added element to his richly mosaic existence along with surfing, theater design, martial arts, ice hockey, cinema special effects, medieval battle re-enactment, photojournalism, Zen archery, scuba diving, motorcycling, Japanese calligraphy, paintgun combat — all components in the adventure that is Scott Huegel's life.

In the two years after Spoke broke up, Scott would graduate from college, move to a country on the other side of the Earth, learn the language proficiently, teach children as a foreign instructor, trot to remote places the world over, and explore subjects ranging from ancient Buddhism to modern socialism. In his travels, he'd meet a wonderful British woman whose lust for life matched his own. The wedding was great.

I often wonder what those high-school administrators, teachers and peers who wrote Scott off as a convict in the making would say of him now. Sometimes I feel like going back to Longwood and rubbing his success in their petty faces.

In his more incendiary moments, I bet Scott does too.

chuck

If a man does not keep pace with his companions, perhaps it is because he hears a different drummer.

HENRY DAVID THOREAU

When Chuck Horne is in full percussive splendor, the rumblings of plate tectonics sound like a sniffle by comparison. With a full rap of the snare, Chuck could break window panes three states away. When he was on, the kid was a machine.

By choice, Chuck's drum kit was pretty ho-hum — a pair of tom-toms, a snare, a bass drum, a floor tom, a high hat and a couple of cymbals — nothing showy, just what he needed to function. For a while he had a cowbell, which I loved because it made us sound like Sheila E., but he eventually discarded it.

Chuck's kit was heavy — spine-cracking, hernia-popping, stroke-inducing heavy. A forklift would've come in awfully handy on some nights. Its upkeep was expensive, too; hammering the living shit out of those skins on a nightly basis, Chuck was constantly having to fix and replace parts. A full-fledged coke habit would've cost less than the myriad drum heads, cymbals, sticks and percussive miscellany he was constantly emptying his pockets for.

Not that he ever had much money to spend. It seems as long as I've known Chuck, he's been able to just scrape by and be satisfied he had anything at all. In high school, for instance, he'd buy himself these crazy 50-cent thrift-store cowboy shirts, real Conway Twitty shit: lasso and floral embroidery at the shoulders, fake mother-of-pearl buttons, metallic collar tips tailored for bolo ties. I guess in the distant future those cowboy shirts may become very chic, in which case Chuck will prove to be quite the fashion visionary. But in 1985, only mass-murderers and Klansmen wore shirts like that.

This caused some trouble for me because Chuck and I looked somewhat alike; even today people mistake us for brothers. Chuck almost slugged a guy who, thinking Chuck was me, jokingly grabbed the front of his hair and jolted his head back. I was always fielding questions on what I was doing in an orange cowboy shirt earlier in the day. Chuck was like my evil twin, only not evil — just weird.

Many classmates dismissed Chuck as a born clown, always ready with a disarming joke to render any serious conversation void. To most girls, he was your average "sweet guy" — innocent, funny, easily heart-broken, sometimes quiet. I, however, found him a little more complicated, long suspecting his goofball nature was partly a line of defense against some turmoil hidden to us all. I caught glimpses of it on occasion, flashes of alienation and subdued rage that came to the surface. Where it came from, I didn't know. In many ways, I still don't.

After high school, things got difficult for Chuck. His parents were divorcing, which, for him, was a matter of bad timing; my parents, as well as Scott's, had also divorced, but we were much younger. With few professional skills, little money for college, and his home life all but disintegrated, he did what a lot of struggling people do. He joined the Army.

"I'll still be the same goofy kid when I come back," he said to me a few weeks before basic training, "hopefully a bit more straightened out."

"Okay," I said.

I thought it was a bad idea. Chuck was essentially a pacifist and nonconformist; the Army didn't seem like a good place for him. But who was I, with my comfy ass snug in a college dormitory paid for by my father, to judge his decision?

In the years to come, during long road trips to out-of-town shows, Chuck would recount in very precise detail the rigors he and his fellow recruits endured in boot camp: the obstacle courses, the tear-gas chambers, the 4:30 a.m. six-mile runs, the fights in the barracks, the not-so-subtle brainwashing. (During marches, the drill sergeant would yell: "What makes the grass grow?" The troops were instructed to respond in unison: "*Blood.*" Chuck's response: "*Chlorophyll.*")

Chuck made it through boot camp and began his Advanced Individual Training in Fort Knox, Ky. That he got through the hardest part with ease didn't surprise me; he's a tough kid, reasonably respectful of authority, and accountable for himself and his associates — all qualities essential to a good soldier. I still wonder, then, what made him crack.

Maybe the very problems he joined the Army to forget were exacerbated. Maybe he felt the military could do nothing to improve his situation. Maybe he didn't like the person they were trying to mold him into. But after six months, he left. He walked off the base and, with the little money he had, took a bus from Kentucky to Florida, where Scott took him in.

I have a photograph of Chuck sitting in a chair shortly after he arrived in Florida, a close-up. He's smiling uneasily and his eyes are tired and tense. It's the portrait of a young man putting up a good front while wondering if his life is gradually coming undone.

Chuck knew he couldn't stay AWOL for long. He had to return to his post and face his superiors in order to be a legal civilian again. Evidently, the Army won't keep a new recruit against his or her will. I'm hazy about the particulars, but if you're willing to bow out with a "general discharge," they're willing to wash their hands of you.

After a few weeks in Florida, Chuck returned to his station. He sat in a chair for three hours as his superiors laid into him, telling him he was a coward, a disgrace. They said if he returned to the ranks, they'd forget the whole situation; otherwise, he'd never be able to find a job again and his shameful retreat would haunt him for life.

But Chuck, who can be pretty stubborn, was resolute. They finally gave in, kicking him out the door with a general discharge and an extended middle finger from Uncle Sam.

Chuck returned to Orlando to piece his life together. He found a job at Toys 'R Us, then a video outlet, subsisting on minimum wage in run-down apartments on the edge of town, spending his every nickel on rent and utilities.

When we asked him to play in a band, Chuck saw the opportunity to wipe his slate clean. On a 98-degree afternoon, with all of his possessions crammed into every cubic millimeter of Scott's car, we sat in bumper-to-bumper traffic on Interstate 75 for four hours from Orlando to Gainesville, nearly overheating the car, melting his prized record collection, and slow-broiling our internal organs. But we got him to Gainesville. He was ours now.

Our first few practices were in a living room kindly provided by our friends P.J. and Christie. They lived in a quiet, gray apartment complex abundant with yuppie students — not exactly prime breeding ground for germinating punk cacophony. P.J. and Christie got complaints.

Because Chuck was more musically skilled and experienced than we were, and because his tastes ran wider than mine or Scott's at the time (Thin Lizzy, Miles Davis, Gary Numan and Slayer were heavy Chuck favorites), he seemed unsure about confining himself to our simplistic 4/4-beat, emo/pop-punk. It didn't help that I all but sermonized on what rhythms to play.

"Chuck," I'd say, "play this kind of beat: *buh-buh-BUH, buh-buh-buh-BUH*...," waving my hands in the air idiotically like I was actually drumming. I never noticed him gritting his teeth.

He put up with this until about our fifth practice, when I said: "Okay, in this part I want you to give me a Jawbreaker-sort of beat." This was an asinine statement, given that Jawbreaker's drummer used lots of different rhythms, none especially characteristic.

Chuck went insane.

"FUCK THIS SHIT! IF YOU WANT A JAWBREAKER BEAT GET THE FUCKING DRUMMER FROM JAWBREAKER! IF I'M GOING TO BE IN THIS FUCKING BAND *I'M* GONNA PLAY *MY* INSTRUMENT *THE WAY I FUCKING WANT!*"

End of practice.

This little outburst only punctuated the fact that, in those first few weeks, we had zero chemistry as a band, lacking any semblance of musical cohesion. Worst of all, Chuck seemed bored, like he came all this way for nothing.

"It's not working out," Scott said to me. "Chuck just doesn't seem into it. It's like playing with us is a chore."

Faced with the very grim possibility of kicking him out, Scott and I drove to his apartment for what was potentially our last practice together, choosing to see how the situation panned out before deciding anything.

On the ride to our warehouse space, Scott and I were tense. Nobody was talking. Nothing was playing on the tape deck. Scott drove silently while Chuck looked out the window, as did I.

Then, still looking at the road, Chuck said:

"Man, I'd rather be doing this than anything else. With all the shit I've been through, with everything that's been going on, this band is the only thing that's given me hope in a long time. It's all I look forward to. I don't care what happens, as long as we keep playing. I'm with you guys, I'm making challenging music, I'm doing something that matters. We're really coming along. The songs are getting better. I can't wait to play."

Scott and I sat speechless, our jaws perceptibly hanging.

"Chuck," Scott said, "what brought this on?"

"I don't know. I just don't want you guys thinking I'm not a hundred percent into it, because I am. A hundred percent."

This was the turning point. True to Chuck, the change of heart was a little unpredictable, but we weren't complaining.

As for his qualms with my dictating the beats, I could see his point. With no say over the songs' melodic structure, Chuck wanted the only element he could provide under his control. So we developed a new way of working: we'd repeat a song segment while Chuck fiddled with different beats, sometimes playing the same chorus or refrain for 20 minutes nonstop. Tedious, yes, but it did the trick.

Chuck soon found a good job at a local record store, proving the threats of his Army supervisors to be garbage. He moved into SpokeHouse after a few months and, surrounded by his friends and bolstered with a heightened sense of purpose, he confidently returned to his old goofball form. Even the city newspaper, *The Gainesville Sun*, took note of it.

"If Spoke were the Beatles," the article began, "Scott would be Paul, Jon would be John, and Chuck would be Peter Tork."

spokehouse

All children are essentially criminal.

DENIS DIDEROT

SpokeHouse was always a mess.

We did our best to keep it tidy. On diligent days, we'd spend hours sweeping and polishing and putting things in order, only to resign ourselves to the tumbleweed-like dust-bunnies that would roll out from behind the furniture across the scuffed hardwood floors, the grimy dishes hidden in closets with a year of foodstuff caked on, and the sea of roaches behind the walls that would occasionally pour onto the outside world, giving us a glimpse of the Roach Nation living among us.

"Fuck this," my roommates and I would declare halfway through cleaning, deciding to spend the rest of the day at record stores for our valiant effort. "Dirt never hurt anybody."

Most towns, especially college towns, can boast a few punk hellhouses, some dumpier than others, falling somewhere between *Little House on the Prairie* and a ghetto junkyard. Among them was the SpokeHouse: an ordinary-looking, 1920s-built structure painted dull white, in its prime it was home to members of three bands (including me, Scott and Chuck, hence the name), nine fanzines, three small record labels and a record/zine distributor. We welcomed touring bands big and small, old friends and distant wanderers hailing from the Bronx to Scotland. We also had a regular entourage of uninvited guests: the doped-up transvestite who traipsed into our living room and pulled down his/her panties while we were studying for finals; the practicing Satanist who took shelter in the house after being punched by her boyfriend on our front yard (she doubted our trustworthiness when she learned we *weren't* Satanists); or the many would-be burglars casing the grounds, who, having taken account of our scant possessions, always moved on to the neighbors.

SpokeHouse sat a block from campus off University Avenue and 13th Street, two main boulevards that dissect downtown Gainesville, on a piece of property valued as highly by hawkish real estate investors eager to exploit the convenient location as by lack-adaisical college students craving the luxury of rolling out of bed into their classrooms down the street.

The most predominant SpokeHouse feature was its large, comfortable front porch with painted red steps leading to the main doors. The porch walls were adorned with fliers of upcoming shows, graffiti written with crayons and black Sharpees ("Fuck Emo"), and brown burn marks around the mailboxes from detonated bottle rockets.

On the steps of the porch, we whiled away our time strumming acoustic guitars at 3 a.m., cussing at friends and cars on the street, giving whatever change or food we had to passing-by panhandlers, and launching bottlerockets at anything that moved. It was the best place in town to watch the hard white sheets of rain fall upon Gainesville's sleepy afternoons, to finish the day's homework while eating cheap lunches from nearby Burrito Brothers or Caribbean Spice, or to smooch girlfriends as a Wedding Present or Arcwelder record blared from inside the house. But above all, amid piles of empty King Cobra and Rolling Rock bottles that sprung in the defoliated bushes alongside the porch, we spent a great deal of time talking shit and doing nothing.

Our landlords — a husband-and-wife team — were among the most oblivious people I've ever met. They took laissez-faire landlording to new heights of neglect. This obviously suited our purposes well: they never balked at our late rent, they remained unfazed by our bouncing checks and, best of all, they rarely came around to snoop. So any damage done to the handsome wood floors — beer-puddle stains, ska-dancing divots, pyrotechnic scars — went unseen, as did the large window that was broken by a hard old piece of pizza crust someone hurled through it, or the living-room French doors that were smashed during an impromptu game of indoor soccer. Though repairs responsible to the landlord went ignored, none of us would dream of complaining. We didn't want them to realize we were turning their house into tinder.

The worst damage came from parties. On my 21st birthday, for example, about 400 people filed through our house to see four bands perform in our living room, an area smaller than a minor-league bullpen. As the bands played at full volume, partygoers trying to dance, drink or socialize were smooshed into a moving, undetachable cluster of flesh and sweat, expanding and contracting over each available inch of floor space. We hunched in a terrified corner and blasted through a quick set of songs, trying to protect ourselves from the blob of humanity as it destroyed everything in its wake.

By the night's end, the final toll was seven windows broken and three skulls gashed (from crowd-surfing too close to the ceiling fan, which ended up busted). The overflowed toilets resembled post-meltdown Chernobyl. The kitchen floor was submerged in an inch of beer, thanks to a broken keg pump. My cat Cleo smelled like the barrel of a '33 Winchester from the ongoing pyrotechnic fiesta outside. And sundry party trash — bottles, cups, hippies — was strewn from one corner of our block to the other. It was impressive.

(From that evening forward, I realized I could kiss my $325 security deposit good-bye — a lesson that has since become something of a lifelong credo.)

For my birthday the next year, the same event was advertised on a lark in the newspaper where I worked, bringing more party-mongers, beer-whores and all-around assholes — including a brigade from the Alachua County Sheriff's Department. I'm sure in the two hours the cops spent waving their billyclubs at us, dozens of muggings, carjackings and miscellaneous acts of lawlessness occurred all over town: "The cops are at SpokeHouse! *Let's go looting!*"

As the first order of business, the police told everybody on the street to pour out "any beer on their person," arresting drinkers under age or without an ID. They then moved people off the sidewalk — "public property," they said — and onto the six inches of space by the side of our house, already occupied by shrubbery. (Pity our trampled, beer-soaked shrubs.)

If these officers really wanted a riot, shoving a few hundred drunk malcontents into a half-foot row was a good way to start one. Chests high and voices gruff, barking orders into megaphones, the cops were no doubt enjoying themselves. Here they were afforded a safe, easy opportunity to flex their authority, a chance to vent the day-to-day frustrations of being a cop on what they believed to be a bunch of spoiled weirdos.

Spending much of the evening jockeying around, informing everyone of the police ultimatum — get inside the house, leave, or be arrested — I can't say I shared their satisfaction. Everywhere I turned, some cop was causing trouble.

"You throw that cigarette at me?" one policeman yelled at a friend who had discarded his spent smoke near the cop's foot.

"No, I was just flicking away the butt."

"Bullshit! You deliberately threw that at my chest!"

"I didn't—"

"You mouthing off? *You want me to take you in, boy?*"

"Take you in" — that was the big phrase of the evening. I had to kiss ass left and right to get people off the hook for doing *nothing*, leaving the cops huffing mad, all adrenaline-surged and wide-eyed and ready to brutalize somebody. Call me naive, but by the end of the night I definitely had a greater appreciation of what folks like N.W.A. were getting at.

Finally an older policeman pulled me by his car. He seemed to be the only sane one present. He told me my party was a "public nuisance," and as the person responsible for throwing it, I had to call it off or else I would be arrested.

"Sir," I began in a tone more honey than vinegar, "if all the people are well-contained in my house and on our property, how could it be a public nuisance?" Where the hell is a card-carrying ACLU law student when you need one?

"Look," he said, "you seem like a pretty reasonable kid. I don't know why you'd want to take the heat for this mess. This is really out of control."

"But if I call this off and you order all these people to leave, that would mean many intoxicated individuals would be on the streets. If they stay longer, they can hang out and sober up. The keg's dry anyway. I mean, is that what you want? Drunk people on the roads?"

Ah, kick him where it hurts. He pondered my rebuttal, unlike the majority of his badge-clad comrades who probably would've tazered me by now.

Yeah, I thought, I'm making progress here, I think they're really going to leave. But before he could answer, from the corner of my eye I noticed something falling from the the sky, a bright green object descending in our direction like a cannonball.

I ducked. When the cop spotted it, it was too late. He had only enough time to yell:

"*Motherfucker!*"

A water balloon launched from the roof of a neighboring punk shit-hole, the Barcelona House, burst atop the police car, drenching the car roof, the police lights, the windsheild...

And the cop.

His demeanor changed instantly. Dripping wet, his face red and his hands shaking, he grabbed my arm and shouted to his troops:

"That's it! We're shutting this freak show down *now!*"

He jerked me by the elbow. "What the fuck was that?"

"A water balloon," I said.

"Don't be funny, asshole."

He poked me hard in the ribs and spoke close to my ear. "If you don't call this thing off, I'm calling in reinforcements," he said, his teeth clenched, his grip tightening on my arm. "And we'll be taking *you* in handcuffs."

Happy 22nd birthday!

The policeman dragged me to a cop car with a speakerphone and handed me the CB. "They seem to listen to you, so tell them to disperse," he said. "Or you're under arrest."

Of course. The Judas blow.

"Um," I began, the speakerphone echoing, "it seems the police have decided not to be too cooperative tonight. They're making me tell everyone to leave or go inside. If you're anywhere on the street, sidewalk or curb, they'll arrest you. They say they'll arrest me if I don't tell you this, and I don't wanna spend my birthday in jail..."

Somebody yelled: "Fuck the pigs!"

"They tell me this is the law," I said, talking fast, "but I don't agree with it, and if you don't either, then maybe you should take action by getting the badge number of any police officer that harasses—"

"Let's cut this short," the cop said, pulling the CB from my hand. So much for my soapbox.

Eventually everyone left, including the police. The next morning, surrounded by endless empty beer cans and spent roman candle cases, I ate the remnants of my birthday cake alone.

This was by no means the last we'd hear from the police at SpokeHouse. From then on they would cruise by between one and four a.m., when we were most active. Because of complaints from grumpy neighbors awakened by our late-night restlessness, we were a regular checkpoint on their beat — "habitual disruptors," trouble with a capital T.

But the only time a cop ever really piped up to us was late one autumn evening, when a guy carrying a six-foot fiberglass Albert the Alligator (the University of Florida mascot) above his head sprinted in front of our porch. Not far behind, a cop car peeled out of the cross-street alley with lights flashing in full chase mode.

The perpetrator dropped the alligator in the middle of the street and bolted. Before giving chase, the cop stopped in front of our porch and bellowed to us over the bullhorn:

"DON'T TOUCH THE GATOR."

When he sped off, we not only touched the gator, we hoisted him 15 feet up a tree in our front yard. A bird made a nest in it a few weeks later.

Surely the most attention we ever received from the authorities was for the infamous "roadkill dummy." Two friends who had moved up from Orlando, Brian Hoben and Ed Ballinger, were moping around our house one night, bored witless. With little else to occupy them, they put together a rag-tag dummy, stuffing old Salvation Army clothes into a throwaway shirt, pants, and socks, even fashioning a "head" from corduroy fabric. They laid the dummy on our front street, where Rob Ray, upstairs neighbor and Paste Eater bassist, splattered red silkscreen paint on the surrounding pavement. As homemade, phoney, blood-strewn corpses go, it was a real work of art.

Since it was nighttime, the dummy looked convincing from afar, and for the next 15 minutes we sat on our porch in hysterics as drivers skidded and swerved to avoid the fake cadaver. One guy even veered up the curb onto a neighbor's lawn.

Then the manager of a nearby restaurant — a friend from my freshman year — arrived at our porch, saying people were coming into his place looking pale and claiming a dead body was in the street.

"Oh, no," I said jovially. "It's not a real body. It's a dummy! We're just playing a little prank!"

He looked at me disapprovingly.

"Tell them that," he said, pointing toward the restaurant.

A loose assemblage of two dozen freaked-out people slowly crept towards us in vacant "must-see-dead-guy" mode. Realizing I'd have to explain this sick and sophomoric joke (which I still find pretty funny) to this traumatized throng, I saw it in my best interest to flee the scene and hide like a wussy.

Everyone followed me into the house. We pretended not to be home as knocks on the door from concerned citizens grew louder. We had to muffle our giggles.

Intermittently peeking through the window shades to see what was going on, we were curious as to how much attention an inanimate traffic casualty would yield. Sure enough, within a span of five minutes, not one police car arrived.

Seven did.

To be exact: seven police cars, two ambulances and a fire truck.

For a dummy.

I was about to hibernate in the oven. There was no way in hell I'd take the fall for this one. Luckily, a friend who was stopping by the house to say hello consulted with the authorities and managed to settle things. He had no idea what he was walking into and knew nothing of the prank. He was also tripping on two hits of acid.

Once the paramedics, firemen and cops ascertained the victim was not human, they left the scene without carting us all to the gallows. (Said one policeman to fellow cops in perfect B-movie dialect: "Nothin' t'see here, boys — let's move 'em out.")

In time, as the parties became more frequent and the property degradation more obvious, our landlords sold the house (at a loss, I'm sure) to a young couple from my native Louisville, Ky. It was evident from the start that our vision of SpokeHouse conflicted greatly with the new owners'. They intended to raise the property value by making it "attractive," building cedar patches, picket fences, flower beds and park benches outside the house.

In all fairness, they had every right to do whatever they wanted, and we thought they were pretty cool at first. They even made an appearance at one of our shows. But because of their lack of tact in confronting us about their plans — as well as their disdain towards us as "undesirables" (a classification they would later present in court, allegedly) — we would, in time, do our best to sabotage their scheme, to delay their self-serving gentrification.

It began when they demanded that we clean the steps of the stairway leading to the second floor. Seeing that we thought the steps were *plenty* clean, we sprayed the stairs with fire-extinguisher foam instead. Why? Because we were a bunch of undisciplined brats who liked living in a hovel and didn't want to be told how to clean up after ourselves? Probably.

Consequently, they tried to get the police to arrest fellow occupant Scott Adams for the "crime." I don't recall whether he had anything to do with it or not, but sending the police after Scott Adams is like deploying an F-16 to kill a horsefly. A man of essentially gentle nature, he was probably the only innocent tenant among us.

We retaliated by shooting bottle rockets from second-story windows at the owners' asses while they weeded cedar patches by the porch, and by writing satirical anti-landlord threats in a plate of wet cement they had laid on the front sidewalk. They called the police, but to their credit, the cops did nothing.

Admittedly, we handled ourselves immaturely. From an ethical standpoint, we knew we weren't doing the right thing. But as it became more evident that our new landlords were intent on flushing us out by any means, doing the right thing seemed a lot less important than doing the fun thing.

After Scott and I graduated from the university, everyone in the house (except Chuck) chose to move out. I had no desire to leave, but with both college and Spoke about to finish, I had no reason to stay.

Upon my departure, it was clear to me that our band would have never fared so well if not for the centrality and warmth of this house. It made us *us*. With our stuff moved and the rooms naked and empty, our time there seemed marked by the scars we were leaving behind.

Each scuff, scrape and hole seemed to have a memory attached to it, a story of how it got there and why. It was very hard to leave.

The owners would ultimately succeed in turning SpokeHouse into a quaint, over-priced dwelling for Young Republicans and sorority presidents, degenerating it into a profitable piece of real estate devoid of spirit and character. I left on such terrible terms with the owners that they supposedly asked the Alachua County Court to issue a 10-day restraining order against me, barring my presence from the SpokeHouse premises because I "constituted a threat to the well-being of the property."

Amen.

amps

The greatest task before civilization at present is to make machines what they ought to be: the slaves, not the masters, of men.

HAVELOCK ELLIS

Make no mistake: despite harmless appearances, guitar amplifiers are dedicated enemies of the human race. Under the guise of volume enhancement, their real aim is to betray, subvert and ultimately destroy each and every one of us.

Perhaps I should explain.

My experience with amplifiers, spanning nearly a decade, has been nothing short of a full-blown nervous breakdown. Though they seem to be reliable machines — reliable enough to bear the brunt of a guitarist's full dependence on them, at least — they're about as trustworthy as a mass murderer at the controls of a ferris wheel, and just as predictable.

I couldn't trust my two amps any farther than I could carry them (which wasn't far, since carrying them was like carrying a pair of bank vaults). When they were supposed to stay silent, they squealed; when they were supposed to thunder, they died. If they had legs, I'm sure they'd kick me in the ass then run. And trying to elicit just the right sound from one — that is, manipulating the degree of electrical response to the guitar's audio signal by way of metered instruments built into the device — is like squeezing milk from lead.

And let's not forget the pummeling our delicately constructed ears take from these machines. The guitar amplifier is to the defenseless human ear what a jackhammer is to a square foot of virgin asphalt, the cumulative effect of which is a long-term inner-ear crumbling. If my left ear takes one more skull-splitting, tube-busting blast from a stack of amps, I'm afraid the poor thing will just fall off.

I played through two Peaveys, the Chevette of the guitar world. One had a rough, overdriven sound, something like an old Dodge without a muffler; the other, a more lush, smooth distortion, like a typhoon wind. On those rare occasions when Jupiter's third moon was in line with Orion by way of the Neptunian Space Veldt, they sounded pretty good. Otherwise, I had problems.

Amps are like humans — moody, flaky, enigmatic. I'd hug them if I thought it would help, and don't think I haven't tried. Nerdy guitar aficionados slobber over "good" amps like a cheap salesman ogles middle-aged lap dancers after a few stiff drinks. But not me. I know better.

Amps are insufferable. They've dicked me over 10 times worse than the most heartless ex-girlfriend; they've turned on me meaner than a rabid Doberman. Their very nature is to humiliate, degrade and mock all of humanity — or, well, maybe just me.

Unfortunately, the amps have us by the balls. Because if you find yourself powerless to fight the need to strum, pick and bash away at those strings, making the most absorbing, glorious din this side of Gabriel's horn, you deal with it. An imperfect machine, you learn to endure its frailties. As with humans, you have little choice in the matter.

audience

Many sensible things banished from high life find an asylum among the mob.

HERMAN MELVILLE

It always surprised me that people would come see our crappy band. Didn't they have something better to do?

In Gainesville, most of the folks at our shows were friends we'd see in the course of a week on the SpokeHouse porch. During our set, they'd just as soon stand listlessly in front of us gulping King Cobras. For out of town shows, devotees of punk's most obscure reaches would make an appearance to satisfy their curiosity, having read a record review in a fanzine or heard our name through the scene grapevine. Usually they'd stare intently as we played, their arms folded, their bodies motionless, analyzing our performance against whatever band we reminded them of that evening.

But from time to time, things got intense. That vital connection, mutually intoxicating between the audience and band, would be made. Some of those nights were really hopping.

Like most punk bands, we'd sometimes find ourselves playing in front of hundreds of kids slamming furiously in a whirlpool of heads, arms and legs. From the stage, this dance-floor action took odd shapes: a high-velocity rugby game, sans ball; a cluster of micro-organisms crawling over each other, darting randomly in all directions, invading all available space; or a well-mannered riot, with smiles amid pogoing and thrashing participants.

Sometimes our only audience was a solitary bartender scrubbing shot-glasses behind a counter, trying his best to pretend we weren't there. Sometimes boys and girls barely on the threshold of puberty were in attendance. Sometimes a few moms and dads were too.

Fortunately, our crowds were rarely overwhelmingly male, so the gals were often in force rocking as hard as the guys. Unfortunately, we never attracted much of an ethnically or racially diverse crowd, which I think was more an unfortunate facet of punk's limited appeal (at least in our part of the world) than any unwelcome attitudes harbored by audience members.

Conversely, large numbers of Nazi skinheads were rarely present either. When Scott, Chuck and I first started going to underground concerts in the mid-'80s, Florida was a hotbed for young fascist thugs. We got in some rough situations, like finding our sorry asses locked — and I mean *locked* — in a warehouse show with 35 belligerent skins ready to beat the stuffing out of us "peace punks." Luckily, by the time Spoke started, skinhead infighting between Nazis and non-racist SHARPs* and independents had taken the wind out of the white-supremacists' sails, which was fine by us.

We never had altercations with Mace spray, knives or guns among crowd members either. How anybody can temper a gunfight from the stage is beyond me, but a few bands have had to do it.

We did have to break up fights now and again, during which a comical metamorphosis took place between me and Scott. Upon the first hint of trouble, we would transform from wimpy, little sensitive guys to Schwarzenegger-turned-Eagle-Scout protectors of the peace. We'd stand up to any antagonist, no matter how large or intimidating, solely because we were on a stage with the power of a microphone, hellbent on keeping our shows as free of hostility and injury as possible. By exploiting this illusion of power, no one could tell that, in actuality, we were big pussies.

Of all the fights, the most memorable bout of violence for me was during a particularly crowded, unruly night at the Hardback. We were playing at floor-level, and some guy — stocky, ugly and obviously shit-faced — was shuffling around less than a yard away from me. He kept bumping into my guitar, messing me up.

I shot him plenty of dirty looks, which would've persuaded any sober person to get the hell out of my way. But this person was definitely not sober, and he didn't get the hint.

I shoved him away to give myself room, which he misinterpreted as an invitation to mosh. He took a few steps back, then launched at me. I jumped out of the way just in time.

He missed me, all right — but not my amps. They toppled to the floor with his fat ass on top.

"Aw Jesus," I thought, our song coming to an abrupt halt. "My amps will never survive this."

I got on the mike. "Hey man, I don't know what your problem is but I think you better get the fuck outta here."

The crowd, maybe 200 strong, cheered in agreement.

Apparently he didn't see my point. He stammered — sweaty, slobbering, reeking of Mad Dog — and screamed two inches in

* Skinheads Against Racial Prejudice

front of my face: "Fuck you — *it's your fault.*"

My fault?

"Fuck off," I said. "Get outta here."

I pushed him out of the way and — in front of everyone — he grabbed my shirt with one hand and cocked the other back, making a fist. It took a moment for my brain to recognize the dire urgency of the situation: *Wake up, Jon — this crazy son of a bitch is going to punch you.*

"WHAT THE FUCK IS WRONG WITH YOU?" I yelled, clenching his throat in my right hand. We glared at each other for one long, homicidal second, not knowing who would hit first. All the while, Chuck continued pounding away behind his drumset, oblivious.

Luckily, I didn't have to think long. Everybody pounced on the guy, bolting his arms back, sucker-punching him left and right. Within seconds he was thrown out the door, like a nightclub scene in a gangster movie. With my amps re-aligned and (amazingly) in working order, we continued playing and had a great show. An angry mob certainly is likable when it's on your side.

I think the reason we consistently attracted such crowds — particularly ones loyal enough to protect me from an inebriated psychopath ready to knock my teeth out — had little to do with our music, which just wasn't that good. Instead, people came to see *what would happen next.* I think a lot of bands could learn from this: if you create an atmosphere in which interesting things can happen, they often *will* happen. What we lacked in musical proficiency, we made up for in showmanship, improvisation, a penchant for embracing the unexpected and a willingness to look stupid.

Take Halloween night, 1992. We dressed as KISS — rather, SpoKISS — and, like all of our gimmicks, it was of the high-concept, low-effort variety. We were about as authentically KISS as the average 10-year-old who, a few hours before trick-or-treating, decides he wants to be Gene Simmons — with similarly half-assed results.

In addition to a 10-minute make-up job with grease paint, we bought cheap black wigs from a nearby drug store. We also added a fourth KISS member, our friend Pat Hughes, to stand in as Paul Stanley. Pat hammed it up on stage with an unplugged guitar, but he looked nothing remotely like Paul Stanley. We didn't have a fourth black wig, so Pat had to wear a '70s novelty rainbow-colored Afro wig that was lying around SpokeHouse. Matched with the disturbingly bad make-up and Pat's big, menacing presence, he looked more like a serial-killing clown.

As Gene Simmons, Scott "breathed fire" with the aid of the "poor-man's flamethrower," spraying a can of WD-40 held near his mouth into a lighter, making a big flame. He also "spat blood" by stuffing a whole jelly doughnut in his mouth and biting into it, forcing the red filling to squirt out. High marks for effort.

Chuck, as Peter Criss, sang "Beth," the sappiest of arena-rock love songs, lip-syncing the KISS version (thanks to a cheap tape player I held to the microphone) while kissing the hands of girls on the dance floor.

As Ace Frehley, all I had to do was play guitar and look cool, which was pretty much impossible because I bought the wrong kind of grease paint, the toxic kind that runs when you sweat and burns the corneas out of your eyes. I couldn't crack open my eyelids to see if I was playing the right notes (I wasn't), if I was singing in the vicinity of the microphone (I wasn't), or if bodies were flying at me from every direction (they were), without my eye sockets feeling like they were full of burning embers.

Despite the abortion that was SpoKISS, everybody continued to come see us. We figured if we couldn't deliver the greatest punk rock in the world, we could at least give people something to talk about the next morning.

We would throw fortune cookies to the crowd and drag the lucky catchers on stage to read their fortune over the P.A. We used a cheap brand of cookies with mystifyingly bad English for the fortunes: *Tiptop news goes ball-ball planting for happy dog eyelash.* Indeed.

We would make toast on stage and toss it into the pit, then invite an audience member to come and smash the toaster with a baseball bat. Or we would encourage everyone to "play along" on a couple of old, cheap Casio keyboards that were distributed to the crowd. Naturally, they too would be smashed in minutes.

Throwing things at the audience was always entertaining. We'd regularly shower people with raw pasta, candy, old clothing, cereal, magazines, albums from Hyde & Zeke Records' 25-cent bin, raw garlic, a football, a phone, money, Taco Bell tacos, shoes, gum, tennis balls, rolls of toilet paper, guitar strings, condoms, Atari 2600 cartridges, packages of ramen noodles, yarn, a vacuum cleaner, ice, coffee beans, stuffed animals, chili powder, books, found cosmetics, bottlerockets, packets of barbeque sauce, a cable TV box and anything else we could rescue from the SpokeHouse garbage, all of which were thrown back at us with unnerving precision and velocity.

In the one instance we tried to transcend common gimmickry and do something truly innovative, we bombed. We were opening for

Quicksand and Surgery at a local club, the Covered Dish. Since Surgery had already assembled their drumkit on stage, we had an idea: Chuck would play at one end of the club by the bar, while Scott and I played on the stage, about 60 feet away.

When we told the soundman (who thought we were a little weird to begin with) of our plans, he was instantly annoyed.

"Look, I already have a hectic night ahead of me," he said, shaking his head.

"Hey, c'mon," I said. "It'll be great!"

"What you guys are proposing is" — he paused, choosing his words carefully — "retarded."

"Where's your sense of adventure?" I said. "Nobody's done anything like it here before. Don't you want to be a part of history?"

"To tell you the truth," he said, "I don't want to have any part of this at all." And he walked away.

So we set up without the aid of a P.A. or soundman. This meant we wouldn't have our instruments evenly mixed through the club's sound system. We would have to blast our amps at near-maximum volume to distribute the sound in the room. Having played many spaces (usually parties) with no P.A., this was nothing new to us.

People came into the club confused. Bill Bryson, the owner, was holding his head in his hands. The bartender looked on with a sardonic smile, as if he were going to get a big kick from watching us eat shit.

In hindsight, it was a great idea. But at a distance of 60 feet, we were hearing Chuck's beats a few milliseconds off, or however fast a beat travels 60 feet. What sounded perfectly in-time to me and Scott was completely off-beat to everyone else in the club — like two of the same records playing *almost* simultaneously.

It must have sounded really bizarre because everyone in the club looked seasick. After five songs, we got the hint.

Many people later congratulated us on the nobility of our failure. Walter, the singer and guitarist of Quicksand, told me it was the greatest thing he'd ever seen a band do and suggested we never do it again.

Bill Bryson was enthusiastic about it too, calling it a "once in a lifetime thing — if you get my drift."

Even the uninvolved soundman came around.

"You guys got real balls," he said.

More balls, it would seem, than brains.

vocals

All bad precedents begin as justifiable measures.

JULIUS CAESAR

My voice sucks.

I'm talking *sucks*.

The sound I make when "singing" could be mistaken for a lion puking into a megaphone. My horrible warbling could pass for the last brays of a dying mule. With throat cancer. After swallowing sewing needles. Dipped in acid.

And yet I get this ridiculous thrill out of singing, even at the cost of destroying an otherwise good song, because there are few things in life cooler than hearing your own voice bellow through a room.

When Spoke began, we decided that, in the spirit of democracy, each of us would sing. In time, because I wrote most of the songs, I wound up singing more. At first I tried to do so with great care at a moderate volume, which gave my vocals an awful, nasally resonance, like the bastard child of Social Distortion's Mike Ness and Psychedelic Furs' Richard Butler. A few brutally honest friends pointed out that this sounded worse than if I just screamed outright, so I started screaming. Those friends then told me to quit worrying about my vocals, that I sounded "fine." But we all know "fine" is a relative term; if it doesn't bite, nauseate or itch, pretty much anything can be "fine."

To top it off, learning to play and sing simultaneously was, for me, like trying to formulate pi to the 12,000th decimal while solving a Rubik's Cube with my toes. But after a year of humming and strumming, I eventually made use of every last brain cell to pull it off.

Chuck and Scott never seemed unhappy with my vocals and were very patient and encouraging. "Just sing," they'd say. Chuck has a great voice, but he didn't like to sing much because it distracted him from drumming. He's the kind of guy who sings in perfect pitch at all times, the bastard.

Scott's voice was on par with mine, but he never let any vocal shortcomings bother him. He sang for fun, and that was that.

Because of less-than-adequate genes, I was not blessed with the golden throat of Naked Raygun's Jeff Pezzati or John Doe from X, or the craggy, cyst-ridden growl of Jeff Ott from Crimpshrine, The Clash's Joe Strummer or the incomparable Tom Waits. No, I'm endowed with a voice that sounds like a cavity-ridden muffler attached to the anus of a flatulent walrus.

And nobody wants to hear that.

hardback

As symphonies are ultimately coordinated motions of atoms, so consciousness emerges from chaos.

P.W. ATKINS

There are many good underground rock clubs in this world, but none better than the Hardback Cafe.

On any given night, you could hear an earful of fury emanating from the Hardback up to three blocks away. Inside, regular patrons, attired in yesterday's dirty laundry and looking a little tired, wasted away the hours lounging, loitering, gossiping, smoking, slamming, playing pool, smooching, reading, watching everybody watch everybody else, screaming chit-chat into each others' ears above the clamor of whoever's playing on stage and, more than anything else, slugging down can after can of King Cobra Malt Liquor.

If there was a pit going on and you lost your footing in the middle of it, you would assuredly be lifted off the floor by somebody nearby. If you were taking a shit in one of the Hardback's all-too-exposed bathrooms, you'd undoubtedly get walked in on. And if you entered the Hardback like you *should* be there, no one would think of charging you admission. (Non-regular patrons — "suits," etc. — paid full price to get in and checked themselves for lice upon leaving soon after.)

The Hardback was a second home for many of us, and in its musty, dark confines we burned through the gamut of human emotions — exhilaration, boredom, sadness, arousal, sickness, ecstacy, bitterness, inspiration — often in the same night. Depression and elation were separated by a thin line at the Hardback, and tripping over it a few times in the course of an evening was inevitable. Still, some of the best nights I ever had were at the Hardback — nights I didn't want to be anywhere else on Earth, nights that damn near changed my life.

The Hardback was amazing because of its open-stage policy: for the most part, anybody could book a show there, set up their equipment and play. Without a stage, light racks, satisfactory P.A., soundman (he was usually at the bar downing King Cobras with everyone else) or high door prices, it was a haven for sub-par local acts (like us) and on-the-rise touring bands, providing an almost perfect venue for no-nonsense, stripped-bare, we-can-do-whatever-the-fuck-we-want rock'n'roll. It was our CBGB's, our Masque, our Gilman Street.

What gave the Hardback its distinction (and its name) was the books (mostly paperback) on its walls when it opened. Anyone could "borrow" a book — Zane Grey westerns and cheap spy thrillers were always in abundance — and return it when finished (though few did). The books eventually disappeared; taking their place (for a while, at least) was a great jukebox with 7-inch selections by Buddy Holly, The Melvins, The Clash, Helios Creed, even us, and a basketball hoop installed in the back.

To many, the Hardback was the archetypical dive: badly lit, hot, cramped, perpetually stinking of stale beer, agonizingly loud, graffitied, smoky and brimming with kooks, all of which somehow brought us great comfort. In the late evening — prime Hardback hours, as shows didn't start until midnight on weekends and ended as late as 5:30 a.m. — the wood floors would be slippery with spilled beer, chairs would break, people would walk out the front door dizzy from being slammed into the poles on the sides of the small dance floor, and old-timers would reminisce drunkenly about the holes that remained in the ceiling from the Jesus Lizard's first Gainesville show, when vocalist David Yow was raised above the crowd and began kicking at the plaster. A fight might break out among the token rednecks at the bar; one of the sound guys — they were both named Rob — might complain about somebody dumping beer into the monitor speakers; and the coin slot on the pool table might take another beating from having eaten yet another customer's change.

There would be stretches of months where the Hardback would host a good show just about every night of the week. Alan, the original owner (who later ran for a city commission seat), usually paid us far more than we deserved for our shows, and I expressed concern that the club would go broke if he paid every band so well. Alan would just smile wryly and say: "We're doing okay."

Pretty much everyone who worked at the club was well-liked, especially Dan, a.k.a. Danarchy, who, besides being a really gregarious guy (and one of the few men who could successfully sport a mohawk and a moustache), has a graveyard tattooed on his belly with the names of various defunct Gainesville punk bands/institutions (Wordsworth, SpokeHouse, et al.) etched on tombstones. This was his way of documenting the scene, and I take comfort in knowing that, in the face of total obscurity, we'll never be completely forgotten thanks to Danarchy's illustrated torso.

As for the Hardback, it too will end up in Danarchy's graveyard, having closed its doors for good in 1999. But if you ever find yourself in Gainesville on a quiet night, I bet you could walk to that snug downtown side street and hear the faint ghosts of cheap amps wailing and cymbals clashing, the echoes of drunken laughter and screaming mayhem and the many other sounds of punk rock joy. These things have a way of lingering.

pierre

**What's good for General Motors
is good for America.**

CHARLES WILSON

For better or worse, mobility is crucial in American society. Without a good ride, getting from point A to point B in our sprawled, freeway-linked nation is a rough proposition, especially with a couple hundred pounds of amps to hoof. Luckily, we had Pierre.

"Pierre" was our name for the white 1985 Pontiac Grand Am that Scott's parents gave him when he moved to Gainesville. Getting good gas mileage and running smooth, it was clean, digital and bourgeois, a car Ronald Reagan would be proud to own (except for the Big Black *Songs About Fucking* sticker on the back windshield). It was indisputably the most un-punk vehicle ever.

My earliest memory of Pierre was after Scott snuck it out of his parents' driveway one evening when we were 16. We cruised around all night and, while returning to Orlando from Daytona Beach at 4 a.m. with some friends in the back seat, played Hüsker Dü's "New Day Rising" full blast on Pierre's mighty stereo. Scott and I beat our heads on the dash at 70 m.p.h. on Interstate 4, screaming the song's refrain: *"New day rising! New day rising!"* Our friends were all nerves, buckled down for what was sure to be their oncoming death-by-careless-driver-and-distracting-passenger, but Pierre got us home fine.

Years later, Pierre proved equally dependable for road trips and out-of-town shows. We'd first fit all of our equipment into the car, then squash ourselves in, enduring cramped muscles and widespread loss of circulation. During long trips we'd fight incessantly over which tapes to listen to, with a John Wesley Harding cassette at the center of our squabbles. Lord knows why Harding's syrupy-sweet, pseudo-folk drivel struck a tender chord in Scott, but if Chuck or I even threatened to throw that horrible piece of shit out the window, Scott would vow to put on something worse, like the Plimsouls.

Pierre took a mighty beating from us, logging thousands of miles in trips to practices and shows, sustaining damages from mishandled equipment at every turn. Yet it still managed to bring us to our destinations unscathed, even if we looked like a carful of country-club stiffs getting there.

Hats off to you, Pierre.

florida

The sun keeps us crazy.

RESTROOM GRAFITTI, MIAMI

I relish the day the cockroaches conquer Florida.

The theme parks, strip malls, souvenir shops, golf courses, prisons, beach resorts, retirement communities — every acre smothered under a sea of roaches.

Humanity should surrender Florida to its rightful species. This variety of cockroach, appallingly large, mean and brazen, sometimes endowed with frightful traits (fangs, mustaches, antlers), is the insect equivalent of the Legion of Doom. If you try squashing a Florida roach with a rolled newspaper, it'll swipe it out of your hand and smack you in the face. Then snicker. It ain't pretty.

And yet, with a shrug of the shoulders, Floridians have accustomed themselves to this nasty vermin as just another of the Sunshine State's rogue inhabitants, not so different from its serial killers, native shit-kickers, oblivious tourists, faux-mermaids, cocaine kingpins, moron surfers, nouveau-riche snowbirds, spooky clairvoyants and Jimmy Buffet wanna-be's. Combined with the region's brutal humidity — the kind where you come out of a hot shower and the air outside is steamier than the air in the bathroom — you get a glimpse into the true soul of "the nation's hangnail:" a sun-fried, mosquito-bitten, air-conditioned, pastel-hued nut house, the weirdest state in the union.

Florida hides many strange and wondrous treasures that we, as Spoke, had yet to witness. So for Spring Break, we resolved to book a state-wide tour to explore the Florida unknown to us — the Florida of cock-fighting, dwarf-tossing, alligator-wrestling and "fried cooter" — and, most of all, to play a few shows. Joined by our jovial chauffeur Scott Adams — heretofore referred by his nickname: "Lackey" — we ventured into the cultural wilderness of our own backyard, a land where the mighty roach still rules.

GAINESVILLE: For our tour opener, a couple hundred people packed into the Hardback, and during Radon's set a local skinhead guy had an epileptic seizure. When he started convulsing on the floor, everybody thought he was just rocking to the music. It took a couple of minutes before someone realized he wasn't dancing, and a few upright citizens dragged him outside where, as he continued to convulse, he began foaming at the mouth and his eyes rolled in his head — too far by healthy standards, his pupils having disappeared, his eye sockets holding what looked to me like hard-boiled eggs. Shortly after, he regained consciousness and went home.

Our performance didn't fare much better. Halfway through the set, one of my amps decided to die, so we were cut short.

ORLANDO: I could always count on three things happening here: a high-energy, full-force show; a confrontation with an old girlfriend from high school, in which I might spend the better part of an evening apologizing for things that happened six years before; and the provincial custom of bombarding us with bondage/S&M magazines on stage, leaving us wading through hundreds of pictures of ugly, naked people in such dignified positions as being spanked with a raw steak while chained to a rack.

This established O-Town tradition began when a local punk house mysteriously found a garbage bag full of *Hogtied, Ropeburn, Held Captive* and similar publications on their doorstep. Initially thrilled, the residents soon grew bored with the magazines and wondered how to dispose of them. They thought of us.

The show was on a Sunday afternoon, a difficult concept for us rise-at-dusk types. The venue was a blues bar called the Junkyard in a strip mall, where "Freaky Deaky" Franklin (or some bluesman performing under a similar psuedonym) played the night before. We were stoked.

As expected, the minute we took the stage we were showered with S&M mags. The members of the audience, few of whom were old enough to drive in daylight, were notably wide-eyed, the girls especially; they rarely had the opportunity to slog through hardcore porn literally up to their knees, I guess. A few girls in front had strategically positioned some especially raunchy pages on my microphone, so that at one point I was singing into the crotch of a naked man gagged and bound to a picnic table while a leather-clad, stiletto-heeled woman stood menacingly over him, pulling his testicles with, of all things, salad tongs.

It was probably for the best that my mom, who lived nearby, couldn't attend this show.

Along with Radon, we played with Adventures in Immortality, a four-piece unit blending aspects of Jesus Lizard, early Dead

Kennedys and latter-era Ministry, and Potential Frenzy, whose '77-style retro-punk recalled early Clash, Buzzcocks and Avengers. The young crowd, full of vim and hormones, set ablaze the Junkyard's dance floor, with many beautiful, 16-year-old punk/goth girls among them, deliciously attired in vampy Trash & Vaudeville-wear or ragged Operation Ivy shirts and skate shorts. In their midst, I felt like a butcher at a petting zoo.

DAYTONA BEACH: Scott's girlfriend Jessica was from Daytona, and with her help we booked a show at a tiny club called Up and Atom's. We were playing with her band Less Than Jake, who, a few years after we broke up, would be the most popular thing to come out of Gainesville since Gatorade.

Less Than Jake blasted through an incredibly fun set, though the small crowd seemed a little unimpressed. That surprised me, since LTJ were far tighter and more polished. I was the only guy up front dancing; in the years to come, that would change by the thousands.

Strangely, the place went nuts for us, thanks in part to a gang of big, boisterous, old-school skater guys who called themselves Team Glug or Team Slug or something. Watching them tear up the small room was like observing a herd of rhinos charge around a china shop. Grateful for the enthusiasm, I yelled into the mike:

"This next song goes out to Team Glug!"

Silence. They all stopped and stared at me, looking mean.

"Uh," I said, "what's up?"

"Not Team Glug," Scott said in my ear, sounding fearful. "Team *Grog!*"

"TEAM GROG! TEAM GROG! That's what I said! *Team Groooooooog!*"

The annihilation festively resumed.

After the show we left for Jessica's parents' house, a few blocks from the shore. Though exhausted, I went to the beach with Vinnie, Less Than Jake's drummer and organizational mastermind, to watch the sunrise, as I never miss a chance to view daybreak on the sea.

Vinnie and I laid on the dunes as we discussed Pez dispensers and Japanese toys, two of his greater obsessions. We soon stopped talking as I started drifting to sleep.

The sky was dark. Sunrise was still an hour away. With my eyes barely open, I saw a small, bright light in the distant sky, like a headlight through a pinhole. It wasn't as far as the horizon, but it wasn't close, maybe a few miles out and a couple hundred feet above the sea. It stood stationary for a long time, then gradually descended in a diagonal path towards the sea. Except for the crashing waves, I heard no sound.

I was too tired to sit up and closely observe it. I just sat back on the dune barely awake, thinking, "Gosh, that's a nice light."

It continued to descend until it was above the surface of the water, where it hovered a while. Then, without moving up or down, it vanished.

It occurred to me this wasn't normal.

"Vinnie?"

"Yeah?"

"Hey, I might've been dreaming here, but... Did you just see something weird?"

"Yeah."

"What?"

"A light," he said. "From the sky. It came above the water."

"Holy shit," I said, sitting up.

"I'm glad you saw it," he said. "I thought I was hallucinating."

"Do you have any idea what it was?"

He chuckled anxiously. "No."

"Some kind of Coast Guard thing, maybe?"

"Maybe."

"A meteor?"

"I don't think it was a meteor. It was too slow and it stayed still."

With some embarrassment, I asked:

"Do you think it was a UFO?"

"I don't know, but it's the closest thing to one I've ever seen."

We let that sink in for a minute.

"Let's get the fuck out of here," I said.

We groggily returned to Jessica's parents' house and fell asleep. The next morning, he and I consulted privately to confirm we were together on this. Predictably, when we told everyone, Scott took it personally.

"Bullshit! Bullshit! You're doing this to freak me out!"

Scott's a rational guy with reasonable insecurities — not counting his big UFO phobia. Being abducted by aliens is his biggest fear. As best as I can tell, he's terrified he'll wake up one night surrounded by gray-skinned, three-foot high, mouthless beings with shiny, black eyes from galaxies beyond, who — thanks to their superior intelligence — want to take him from this planet, put him in a "space zoo," perform unspeakable experiments on him, and surgically implant extraterrestrial tracking devices (made of some material "not of this Earth," of course).

He read a book called *Communion* by Whitley Streiber, which is what brought on these visions. Whether valid or not, the extent of Scott's fear grew quite comical. It got to the point he couldn't even look at cartoons of aliens.

"People shouldn't be drawing that shit," he'd say.

He especially hated movies about alien kidnappings, particularly the *Fire in the Sky* variety, where evil cosmic life forms nab unsuspecting campers, forest rangers and roving cows and shove intergalactic space probes up their asses. Scott *really* didn't like the thought of that.

Sometimes he'd stay awake late into the night, locking doors and staring out windows, wondering if he was next. We didn't ease his nerves any: local newspaper clippings about UFO sightings in the area were instantly taped to his door, and occasionally we'd shine flashlights in his window after he went to bed and whisper his name in a creepy "alien" tone.

He figured this "light above the sea" thing was no different.

"You just want me to think they're following us!" he said. "No! Aliens are NOT on tour with us! *Why do you do this to me?*"

FORT LAUDERDALE: Cancelled. The roof of the garage where we were supposed to play collapsed.

MIAMI: With your first big breath of Miami air, you can actually smell the drug money, of which there was plenty circulating, especially in Miami Beach. What I mistook for the brackish sea breeze was in fact floating molecules of cocaine and dollar bills in the air, combined with the occasional waft of freshly spilled blood and gunpowder. All of South Beach looked like it was on coke; even the neon in storefront windows has that suspicious extra "glow." (Or maybe I've just seen *Scarface* too many times).

Then there's Miami Beach's staggeringly high concentration of beautiful people, the sort of Perfect Human Specimen who march off the pages of *Vogue* or *GQ* and converge at upscale dance clubs and bistros at night, looking "fierce," "fabulous" and "smashing." By contrast, I felt like a leper.

Added to the city's intrigue is the abundance of Spanish spoken there. In some parts of town, if you closed your eyes, you'd swear you were in San Juan or Havana or Port-au-Prince. An inability to speak the language in Miami would likely be a problem, and the only Spanish I know is *huevos rancheros* ("ranchers' eggs," whatever those are), *la langocita vomita* ("the little lobster vomits") and *chinga tu puta madre* ("fuck your bitch mother"), which didn't get me far.

We played Miami once before at a sports bar called the Blue Marlin. Wordsworth, Bombshell and Radon were also on the bill. About 250 kids came. Surrounding the stage were TVs tuned in to every hockey game on the continent, plus Budweiser banners and baseball trophies — not exactly our element. The soundman, who bore a striking resemblance to the balding lead singer from Quiet Riot, had the aptitude of a month-old corpse. At one point he left the club completely — nostrils were a little short on blow, I reckoned — with no one to mix the soundboard. So I did it, and I know dick about soundboards.

The owner of the place had the charm of a used-car salesman turned child pornographer. He'd introduce each band like a Reno emcee. Since we were "headlining," we went on last, by which time most of the under-18 crowd had to get home by curfew. Unfortunately, this didn't stop the owner from taking the mike and...

"All right ladies and gentlemen, the band you've all been waiting for... Let's give a big Miami welcome to — SPOOOOOOKE!"

The only people left were a handful of our friends from Gainesville and they were laughing.

Because Dave from Radon had played through my guitar set-up before our set, my ever-moody amplifiers decided they'd had enough for the evening. I never heard such relentless howling and screeching from them. Combined with the bar's terrible acoustics, we sounded like a continuous 30-minute train wreck.

Then, in keeping with the glorious mood of the evening, the owner tried to stiff us for cash, claiming he couldn't pay a dime because of "room expenses."

"Hey, what's the big deal?" he said sitting in his cramped office, a saccharin smile stretched across his over-tanned face. "It's all fun, right? I'll tell you what, we'll lock the doors and you can drink all the beer you want. Our own private party!"

Since I didn't drink, this meant nothing to me. "Listen," I said, barely containing myself, "I know you're running a business here. I know you have certain financial considerations to keep your business alive. I respect that. But we just spent $30 in gas per car to play the worst show in memory. More than 200 kids paid seven bucks a pop to see our bands play. You collected almost $1,500 in one night because we were here. You are going to pay us some of that goddamn money."

He shook his head. "Sorry, guys," he said, still smiling like a jackass. "No can do."

Jason, Bombshell's drummer at the time, a congenial guy only occasionally prone to disorderly behavior, was in the office as well.

"I think it's time to clean this place out," Jason said.

He meant rioting, smashing the bar to bits, making up for lost earnings with destructive satisfaction. It was worth mentioning if only to see the sudden look of alarm on the owner's face, removing that sickening smile.

"You're fucking us," I said. "And if you had any self-respect, you'd admit you're fucking us. Unless you do something to vindicate yourself right now, I'm going to make it clear to every contact I have and every band I know not to play here, because you'll fuck them too."

Yeah, like that was a big threat. What did he care? As a result of my balls-to-the-wall tirade, the owner yielded a measly 20 bucks to each band, which in our disgust and late-night exhaustion we took. Some vindication.

But that was long ago, and we now arrived with a new attitude and a new contact — Jorge from Cell 63, a band unafraid to flaunt its early Replacements influence — and a fine venue: the somewhat legendary club Churchill's in Little Haiti.

The first day, Brent from Radon, Jorge and I went snorkeling. We swam far from the South Beach shore for almost two hours in the clear, jade-like water under the beaming sun. While the array of fish and underwater plants had me transfixed, my wimp-ass body couldn't take the physical exertion of constantly swimming against the choppy tide, so I dog-paddled back to shore.

As I stood up, I felt the skin on my back scream. I was burned like a spent match.

The rest of the day I gingerly nursed my skin with aloe and listened to Jorge's many recorded versions of the dreamy 1955 lullaby, "Sleepwalk" (originally performed by Santo & Johnny). I also watched a few of his strange videos with Lackey (who was coming down with a rough flu), including a Japanese animé feature in which a pubescent Manga girl is raped by an alien monster who, with hundreds of octopus-like penile tentacles, invades her every orifice — including, at the very end, her nostrils. This made us sicker.

Late that night, after watching *The Exorcist* at Jorge's, Brent painted his face white and, using a camera flash for illumination, effectively recreated a creepy, ghoulish visage from a part of the movie that Scott had been too terrified to watch. Brent did this while Scott was almost asleep on the floor, crouching about six inches from Scott's face.

Scott's reaction was classic.

"YOU SICK FUCKERS THINK THAT SHIT'S FUNNY BUT I SWEAR TO GOD IF YOU DO THAT SHIT AGAIN I'M GONNA START SWINGING AND I CAN'T BE HELD RESPONSIBLE FOR MY ACTIONS WHEN I'M BEING FUCKED WITH IN MY SLEEP!"

Scott curled up in his sleeping bag clutching a hockey stick.

The next night was our show. I ate Churchill's world-renowned shepherd's pie, watched some Haitian guys fight with pool cues, and met our soundman Rat Bastard or Rat Fink or Rat Something — the guy who was in Scraping Teeth, voted "Worst Band in America" by *Spin* magazine. I also listened to a kid in the parking lot bash out Samiam's "Too Many Buttons" on an acoustic guitar, which was enjoyable, but our performance overall was mediocre. Ah well.

Back at Jorge's after the show, we got this psychotic craving for pie. We trekked all over Miami looking for any kind of pie, finally scoring a cherry-filled supermarket brand at 4 a.m., gobbling it in three minutes flat. We spent the next hour nursing stomach aches and trying to go to sleep, wondering why we were so suddenly obsessed with eating a pie in the first place.

Lackey's flu worsened. So did my sunburn. Another show fell through, so the only date left was Tampa.

TAMPA: Not exactly Tampa, but Sarasota, which is a good hour away, though as far as I'm concerned it's all Tampa — St. Pete, Clearwater, Bradenton, Venice, the whole Gulf coast. We've had some amazing shows in this area, the Assuck gigs at Blue Chair Records in Ybor City being the standouts, where the local kids did this imploding black-hole thing — simultaneously falling on their backs en masse, the entire pit collapsing in on its center.

Some friends at the Ringling School of Design organized a concert with a few other bands at a large warehouse in town. As we drove there, an ominous storm began brewing, foreshadowing trouble.

A few hundred people representing all shades of Tampa-area counter-culture — punks, art students, hippies, bikers, pagans, skinheads, b-boys — were present. Throughout our set, the infamous Sarasota/Bradenton posse — a group of 20 hyper-creative, dyed-haired, straight-edge skater guys, none of whom looked over the age of 15 — lavished upon us an assortment of strange gifts onstage: stuffed animals, Valentine balloons, fake flowers and a bag of glitter reserved for dumping on me. It wasn't the fine, speckled dust of second-grade art projects; this was the big, confetti-like variety with pointy, prickly edges. Since I wasn't wearing a shirt (the sunburn made it too painful), much of the glitter stuck to my sweaty, irradiated back, creating a discomfort unsurpassed to this day.

Though the warehouse party continued after our set, we decided to split to Bill Crump's house on the Gulf, which he shared with other Ringling students. Lackey, whose flu was taking on ebola-like proportions, bowed out for his parents' house in Bradenton.

As we packed our stuff, the downpour grew worse. Even by Florida standards, where short outbursts of torrential rain are a daily occurrence, this was exceptional. To get to Scott's car in the flooded parking lot, we had to trudge our equipment through 16 inches of water, which started leaking inside the warehouse. Wires connecting the soundboard to the P.A. system were a few inches underwater, as were some power strips.

Driving to Bill's was like a scene from a disaster movie. The downpour was blinding; the wind toppled branches; garbage spread all over the street; hail began to fall. But all I could think about was taking a shower and getting that infernal glitter off my flesh.

Having made it through the meteorological chaos, I removed my wet clothes and jumped in Bill's shower, where I immediately clogged the drain with glitter and overflowed the tub. It took an hour to pick it all out and dry the floor. I was exhausted.

For the sake of my sunburn, I opted to sleep without a blanket, lying on a towel on Bill's bedroom floor and wearing nothing but boxer shorts. As I slept, the weather got *worse*, with the temperature dropping from 75 to 35 degrees. I awoke with the howling wind early in the morning — along with a sore throat, a cold sweat, an immobilizing headache, a rib-crushing cough and the pinch of a few stray pieces of glitter stuck in my butt crack.

Local weathermen, never at a loss to exagerrate, would call this night "The Storm of the Century" — and it was our shit luck that we'd find ourselves in the middle of it. But we weren't nearly as bad off as Lackey: his parents' house flooded with three feet of water. Still sick with the flu, he spent the night with a bucket bailing out his bedroom.

We split our resources. Scott drove the equipment back to Gainesville with Jessica while we took charge of rescuing Lackey. Or rather, Chuck took charge; he had to scoop my feverish carcass into the car and slap me now and again so I wouldn't fall into a coma.

If you've ever seen TV footage of a hurricane breaking on a coastal town, you'll have an idea of what we drove through. Chuck swerved around highway signs falling off their posts onto the street and downed power lines whipping around the flooded pavement. The morning sky was filled with mean, black clouds moving hurriedly across the horizon, with big, hard raindrops falling vengefully.

Lackey was glad to see us. He looked like shit. Chuck and I found this tragically funny. Here he kindly offered his assistance on our little state tour, and we rewarded him with influenza, the worst weather of the century and 24-hour flood patrol.

In Chuck's capable hands, we made the three-hour trek to Gainesville safely. As he swayed and swerved to miss oncoming debris, I managed not to vomit on him. Later, as we stopped at a McDonald's to give Chuck a rest and load up on fries and soda, I observed the many concerned drivers looking worriedly out the windows over their half-eaten Big Macs, wondering if they'd make it through the storm.

Only one seemed undisturbed by the weather, the mood or much else. All he cared about was eating a dropped fry in peace and not getting stepped on. Everything else he could handle.

Goddamn these roaches. They'll outlive us all.

tuned

Man is a tool-using animal. Without tools he is nothing. With tools he is all.

THOMAS CARLYLE

Nothing's quite as unnerving as two high-powered musical instruments playing the same song slightly out of tune. It produces the sonic equivalent of "sour stomach." Think of two airhorns in a duel. You get the idea.

In the case of me and Scott, our tone-deafness could rival a retirement-home sing-along. Between the two of us, we had as much natural pitch calibration as a sack of gravel. That's why we relied so heavily on our smallest piece of equipment, the Li'l Geek, a $60 digital Sabine tuner about the size of an old 8-track cassette.

Once plugged into a bass or guitar, the red and green dots on the Li'l Geek's light board registered whether each string was tuned properly. This was possible thanks to an incomprehensible array of micro-circuitry packed inside the casing. Assuming the 9-volt battery that powered it was fresh, it could tune a blender to a perfect F-sharp. It came as no surprise to us that "real" musicians used the Li'l Geek too, like Bonnie Raitt and The Guy Everybody Used To Call Prince Until He Lost His Mind And Changed His Name To A Hieroglyphic.

I can't remember why we called it the "Li'l Geek" — probably an homage to the second most important device in our lives, Scott's old car the Li'l Hog — but the name belied its importance. On those rare occasions when the Li'l Geek was out of commission or forgotten, Scott and I would have to make do with our own powers of intonation — which, as mentioned, are nil. I'd tune my guitar with this pathetic little harmonica-like tuning horn, and Scott would tune off me, and by the time he got it right my guitar would be out of tune again — all in front of an impatient audience.

As human beings, we seldom take the time to regard the importance of the smaller items upon which we're so dependent, and almost never pay tribute to their significance. House keys, aspirin, pencils, Kleenex, paper clips, razor blades, coins, rubber bands, buttons, safety pins, Li'l Geeks — they're the diminutive, seemingly unimportant things that bring order to our lives. The monumental Sabine tuner, though no bigger than the palm of my hand, allowed us to flourish where we would have otherwise failed.

punk rock

In a lot of ways, we spend our last 50 years getting over our first 12.

STEVE ALBINI

When I was 11 years old, I believed I was the subject of a terrible experiment.

It was late 1981, and I was convinced I was a human guinea pig bred and imprisoned in a carefully constructed environment designed to cause me continuous anxiety.

The experiment administrators, I believed, were people who lived in a Perfect Society where pain, chaos and injustice didn't exist. Curious about such things, they constructed a world of war, disease and injustice — not to mention an unending array of nuisances (boiled cabbage, Don Rickles, post-nasal drip) — and plopped one of their own (me) into this "cage" to see how a person would hold up under such deplorable circumstances.

I don't know how I came up with this idea, but I couldn't shake it. To my thinking, the world was too painful, confusing and altogether fucked-up to be anything but a total fabrication created by pathologically inquisitive scientists from some distant Utopia. I believed every stimulus I was subjected to was carefully scrutinized; what I saw on the TV screen, in newspaper headlines, on the streets — it was all rehearsed and presented by Them, the experiment administrators. What I was taught in "schools" was what They wanted to shape my mind into, and They took great pains to closely monitor my intellectual development. (Needless to say my grades weren't too stellar that year.)

I believed my family and friends were carefully selected actors who literally lived their roles, updating and rehearsing back in the Perfect Society when I didn't see them. And the events of my day-to-day life — where I went, who I talked to, what I said, ate, broke, lost, felt — were recorded and made public to the people of this painless society, who were well aware of my ins and outs like I was a sitcom. They would see all of the foolish mistakes I was making and would laugh at how badly I was coping in this preposterously horrible world. Everyone was in on the joke but me.*

I also developed the idea that some people from this Perfect Society believed the experiment had gone too far and felt compassion for my plight. They wanted to free me, but I figured as liberators they had to keep their efforts discreet. I was always searching for those renegades who had broken into my world to take me back. Somehow I deduced they were disguised as winos and vagrants, of which, in downtown Louisville, Ky. (where my mom and I lived at the time), there were plenty. Consultations with these "saviors" proved memorable, to say the least.

Tormented with this knowledge, I also wondered if, in the event I was freed from this hell I was born into, I could ever adapt to the Perfect Society, having grown so used to my own world, shitty as it was. I obviously kept these thoughts well-guarded, lest They realize I was catching on. I asked myself: How long could They keep this crazy experiment up? Would They one day decide They had learned enough about how much shit a human being can take, then pop into my world saying: "Surprise, Jon — we were just testing you! It was all a joke!"

I was 11 years old and *I was sure of it.*

Maybe my disengaged outlook is attributable to psychological factors: the fragmentation of my tender consciousness by electronic mass media; my constant fear of nuclear annihilation (which, with Reagan as president, didn't seem like such an impossibility); the divorce of my parents when I was four; or simply the anarchistic imagination of an introspective, self-centered single child.

And maybe this outlook would've blossomed into something menacing in the coming adolescent and adult years, perhaps landing me in gutters, padded cells or penitentiaries all over.

But that's hypothetical. Where this outlook came from is still a mystery to me, but how I got rid of it isn't.

It began with a record. An album that belonged to, of all people, my father. It was fun, fast and loud, reckless and spastic and dumb. I listened to it every day. It made me feel great.

It was *End of the Century.* It was by The Ramones.

Shortly after, I bought *London Calling* by The Clash with some Christmas money, and a guy at school taped the Dead Kennedys' *Fresh Fruits for Rotting Vegetables* and the Circle Jerks' *Wild in the Streets* on a cassette for me.

The windfall then began.

---

*If this sounds a lot like the movie *The Truman Show*, you can just imagine how much I freaked when I saw it.

In the decade to come, the songs of hundreds of such bands would comprise the soundtrack of my life. My experiences were marked by the music of widely known groups like Minor Threat, X, Bad Brains and the Misfits, as well as legions of forgotten, overlooked or short-lived acts. They were bands that required deep digging to find, whether through the back pages of fanzines, from tracks of very limited compilation albums, in the recesses of 7-inch racks in dusty record stores, or from cassettes recorded by friends.

They were bands who, from their first songs forward, grabbed me by the throat and pinned me to the wall. Bands like the Mau-Mau's, Teen Idles, U.X.A., Man Sized Action, Really Red, Adrenaline O.D., Social Unrest, Ill Repute, Toxic Reasons, Decry, F, Life Sentence, D.I., Los Olvidados, Verbal Assault, Code of Honor, Proletariat, R.K.L., Blatant Dissent, Adolescents, B.P., Christ On Parade, Angry Samoans, Borscht, Ism, China White, Offenders, S.O.A., Doldrums, Pagan Babies, Aggression, Channel 3, Void, Justice League, Articles of Faith, Free Beer, White Flag, The Freeze, Roach Motel and many, many more.

We all learn our place in the world, where and how we fit in, who we are. I happened to learn through a kind of music, a raging and uncompromising kind, the ideas expressed in it and the community it spawned.

Strange though it may seem, I greatly credit punk rock for putting the arena of my existence in proper perspective, allowing me to unravel the Perfect Society, rid myself of my imaginary tormentors and face reality: I was as entrenched in the human condition as anyone else. My senses shaken and my identity unshackled, it was through the hard sensibility of punk that I found my bearing in this murderous, unjust, back-breaking world of ours.

How lucky I was.

hazards

Effort is only effort when it starts to hurt.

JOSE ORTEGA Y GASSET

Few consider the serious risks that go into crafting noise, a veritable minefield of hazards. For instance, there's...

HEARING LOSS: Human ears haven't evolved to handle the high-decibel assault of modern music. During practices, my hammered eardrums would be (literally) screaming for mercy; it's a miracle I can still hear a whisper without the aid of a megaphone. I don't know how people can play teeth-shattering noise for years without developing some hearing loss, even with ear plugs; as it is, I still go to sleep with scores of little sirens, buzzes and tones blaring inside my head. Unless future medical technologies come up with something miraculous, I can look forward to being as deaf as a rock in my twilight years.

ELECTROCUTION: During concerts, with all of the thrown and spilled beverages, sweat and spit splashing around amplifiers, P.A. equipment and electrical outlets, it's amazing no one gets fried, particularly people in the band. At a really high-temperature show (e.g., old Gainesville house parties), you'll find the band and audience mired in puddles of a vile beer/water/sweat concoction — "gig run-off" — making them perfect human conductors for any stray voltage that might fall their way.

Once, while setting up before a show in Pensacola, I tripped on some wires and somehow landed two fingers directly inside the AC socket of an electrical strip. I saw a quick red flash and my whole body jolted, like squeezing a body-sized joy buzzer. Luckily it didn't take much of a toll, not counting the lightning bolts that occasionally shoot from my nipples.

HERNIAS: Charles Atlas has nothing on punk rock. With each piece of our equipment weighing something like 350,000 lbs., it was inevitable that one of us would get a hernia, and it ended up being Chuck. In his hernial state, Chuck learned that the real burden of a hernia is not the painful operation, the unsightly lump in one's groin

A
M
P
E
D

or the general mental discomfort of knowing that some of your bowel has slipped into your scrotum. No, according to Chuck the real problem is that the word *hernia* sounds too much like a word of even less appeal.

"I tell girls I have a hernia," Chuck told me, distraught. "They'd think I said 'herpes' and run away."

MIKE LIP: This happens when the band is playing on level ground or a low stage. Crazed audience members come crashing into the microphone stand in mid-mosh while the defenseless guitarist or bassist is singing, plunging the mike into the musician's mouth with the force of a George Foreman right-hander. The outcome: swollen lip, plus an occasional busted tooth, bleeding gums, severed tongue, crushed tonsils, battered adenoids, shattered cheekbones and, in rare instances, complete frontal lobotomy. The mike's usually okay though.

BLOODY FINGERS: If you play your guitar too hard for too long, the nickel strings may cut your fingers the way an egg-slicer cuts a hard-boiled egg. You bleed slightly; it hurts. If you continue to play with the wound unhealed, your fingers eventually become infected, intensifying the bleeding so that your guitar and fingers get bloodier with each performance. Anybody watching will instantly assume you are a certifiable punk guitar god, especially when your hand develops gangrene and falls off.

TOPPLING DRUMMER: I've only witnessed this maybe three times in more than a decade of attending rock concerts. Positioned too far to the rear of a high, narrow stage, the drummer just falls off the platform. Invariably it happens in the middle of a song, with the drummer toppling in a comical, cartoon-like frenzy with feet and drumsticks flying in the air. A true showstopper, usually everyone's laughing but the drummer, who's spread on the ground below, totally befuddled, suffering a broken collar bone.

dump

To what purpose is this waste?

MATTHEW 26:8

Chuck, Scott and I had very distinct defecation habits. I, for one, always jumped in the bathroom the minute before we headed out to practice, which meant everyone had to wait up to a half-hour until I finished. I considered it my God-given right to take my sweet time with such matters, hemorrhoids be damned.

Chuck was afflicted with a stress-related condition commonly known as "show turd:" five minutes before you take the stage, your guts get heavy with a voluminous, sloppy mass of blowout. Being near a toilet becomes singularly important, as show turd cannot be fought; you *must* unload *at that moment.* Chuck often staggered around looking for a usable toilet, one without mysterious or unmentionable liquids all over the seat, one without people loitering in the stalls (or worse, necking), and one with something that could pass for toilet paper (as these tended to be messy affairs), usually mere minutes before performing.

Having been stricken with the grim reality of show turd myself, I can attest to the horror of not being able to find a suitable lavatory (e.g., a dark corner of an alley). Once Chuck and I had to resort to the private restroom of a used bookstore owned by a very compassionate Cuban guy. He seemed to know misery when he saw it, and I guess he could tell from the desperation on our faces that we had a problem. We later left him with many relieved thank you's and a bookstore smelling like a stockyard, probably for the rest of the month.

But of the three of us, Scott has the most incredible defecation experience, the kind that could almost be made into a national holiday. Scott has a — well, I guess you'd call it a gift — for extraordinarily forceful flatulence. When he lets one fly, the surrounding atmosphere splits; air molecules just can't get out of the way fast enough.

During one practice, Scott was in the process of releasing some intestinal pressure, which I guess was well up his digestive tract because (as he later told me) he had to help it along with an extra "push." All I saw was a strange look on his face — in retrospect, panic — before I looked away to attend to my amp, which of course was giving me problems.

"J-J-Jesus Christ!" he shrieked.

I turned around and saw him staring incredulously at what appeared to be a pile of refried beans on the floor.

"That's my shit!"

I looked at him, then looked at it. I didn't make the connection.

"That's from me!" Scott yelled. "I JUST SHIT IN MY FUCKING PANTS!"

Well.

At first I didn't believe him, because the logistics seemed impossible: there was no evidence of it on his legs and his shorts were clean. But when he explained how the excrement fired out of his system like a shot from a cannon, too fast to soil skin or garment, it seemed more plausible. Plus, there *was* this pile of shit laying on the floor, even if I found it highly suspect that it came from Scott.

"Where the hell else would it come from?" he said. "The sky?"

Chuck and I looked at each other worriedly. We didn't want to reprimand him for infantile bowel control, but we didn't relish the thought of him making a nightly habit of this either. Not knowing what to do, we just sort of stared at him.

"What?" Scott said. "Why are you guys looking at me funny? You think I'm fucked up or something?"

"Well," Chuck said matter-of-factly, "you *did* just shit in your pants."

So with a deep, primordial disgust, Scott cleaned his little mess and we resumed practicing, teasing him for the rest of the night about his "12-gauge guts." To his credit, rather than let it worsen any pre-existing neuroses, Scott quickly shrugged off the incident, recounting it many times to close friends as a freak event from which he learned a very important lesson: *Never force that which need not be forced.*

I just wish it happened on stage.

walterboro

The road up and the road down is one and the same.

"You boys with the Grateful Dead?"

I looked over the counter at the attendant, wondering who he was talking to.

"What do you people call yourselves?" he said, staring at me. "'Deadheads?'"

"Huh?"

"Over there." He pointed outside by the gas pump at the 1969 blue Volkswagen bus we were touring in. "Ain't that one of them Grateful Dead-following vans?"

"I don't know what you're talking about," I said.

"You're not a Deadhead?"

"Nope."

He shook his head. "Shoulda known. Y'ain't got that long hair and stanky smell. Forty-two cents is your change. Have a nice day."

I climbed back into the van where Scott and Chuck were waiting with Wyatt Roberts and Bill Crump. They were packed in with our rickety equipment en route to the foreign, savage lands north of Gainesville on our first out-of-state tour.

"Got my Snickers?" Wyatt asked. Aside from being our tour driver, bodyguard and interim "spiritual advisor," Wyatt's most important role was that he owned the van, which had already logged a hefty 250,000 miles. He was also a former basketball scholarship recipient at Stetson University, so playing ball against him sucked.

"Thanks," he said, grabbing the Snickers from my hand. "Get your stinky butt in the van and let's go."

I closed the side door and crawled over Bill in the backseat.

"The tour hasn't started and already you smell like shit!" he said as I passed over him.

"You're wrong," I said. "The guy in the gas station said he knew I wasn't a Deadhead because I don't have that stanky Deadhead smell."

"Yeah," he said. "You smell worse."

We had known Crump since high school, when he was a hipster guy who wore paisley shirts buttoned to the collar (a forgotten fashion relic of the 1980s) and listened obsessively to R.E.M. (pre-*Life's Rich Pageant*). At the time of our tour, Bill was studying at the esteemed Ringling College of Art, where he spent his days sunning his long, lush brown hair on the Sarasota beaches for all of the Tampa Bay girls to fawn over. We figured his magnetizing effect on women might come in handy on tour, but it didn't.

Our first show was scheduled the following day in Wilmington, N.C., but as fate would have it, we got hungry half way up and stopped at a Burger King off Interstate 10. As we drove down the exit ramp, a sign informed us that we had entered a town called Walterboro, S.C. It should have read "*Abandon all hope ye who enter here*," but highway signs never tell you what you really need to know.

Having spent a good eight hours cooped up in the van, I stretched my legs and browsed the local overpriced firework boutiques. When I met the guys back at the Burger King parking lot, their mood was grave; some linkage thing broke between some carburetor thing somewhere underneath the van, or something to that effect.

Obviously I don't know shit about cars. To me, both axles could have been severed and I wouldn't have known the difference. But Wyatt, an automotive Encyclopedia Brown, inspected the underside of the van and ingeniously fixed the problem with the E string of my guitar and some duct tape.

We cheered, anxious to leave this foreboding place. But as he drove in circles in the Burger King parking lot, unable to shift the van out of second gear, our elation seemed premature.

Again: I know nothing about cars. But I knew if Wyatt couldn't get out of gear, the transmission was *kaput*, meaning we were screwed.

After parking the van in the Burger King lot, Wyatt and I sought the services of a mechanic down the road. It was dark and chilly, and the dimly lit alley that led to the repair station was pitted with massive potholes holding rainwater and motor oil, eerily reflecting the fluorescent lights of the garage.

The two guys working the station were about our age, maybe a few years older. They wore overalls with no shirts and squarish, black baseball caps embellished with auto-parts brands on front. They sported weak, nearly transparent mustaches, and wiped their blackened hands on rags already saturated with grease.

My first thought was to whisper a lame hick joke to Wyatt: "These guys look like siblings — I bet their parents are, too." But I saw no point in worsening our potentially shitty karma just to flaunt some snide metropolitan prejudice.

They hauled the van up on one of those Giant Steel Hydraulic Flatbed Things. I've never had the guts to inspect the bottom of my car while it was jacked up on one of these unsturdy-looking contraptions, since I'd probably be the unlucky one-in-a-billion collapsing hydraulic-flatbed casualty, my entire spinal column flattened to a stubby three inches.

After poking around under the van, grunting affirmatively throughout, the boys returned with a verdict.

"Ain't nothing we can do," one said. "Transmission's broken."

"That I know," Wyatt said.

"There is one person who can help you," the other said. "Tammy."

"Who's Tammy?"

"She's the local VW expert. She can fix it."

"How can I get a hold of her?"

"Not till morning. She don't fix cars at this hour."

"Wait a minute," I intervened. "You mean we're going to have to stay the night here?"

"Guess so." In the distance I think I heard a scream.

We found lodging at the nearby Thunderbird Inn, one of those highway motels constructed for:

- elderly couples on their way to time-shares in Florida.
- unmarried couples (at least to each other) in need of a private place to indulge their carnal desires.
- punk fucks shit out of luck (like us).

That night we watched a few hours of depressing TV including a news special about the worldwide spread of AIDS, which didn't brighten our mood. Eventually I fell asleep on the floor, blanketless, to the sound of trucks hauling ass down I-10.

Wyatt woke us at dawn. He contacted Tammy and was excited. I, however, awoke very, very slowly. Mornings rarely greet me with much happiness, and the whole concept of "rise at dawn" is an ordeal I try to avoid.

"Get your ass in gear!" Wyatt said as I waddled by, my eyes still shut. I barely had the energy to reply: "Fuck off."

Two tow trucks waited in the Thunderbird Inn parking lot — one to carry us, the other to carry the van. We happened to get lucky and ride in the one with the bulldog and the chihuahua.

"Them's my dogs," the driver said. "Get on in. They won't bite."

Crump sat next to Bozo, the bulldog, whose lower two fangs protruded above the jowls hanging over his mouth. Bill isn't exactly a bulldog kind of guy — he's more of a Snoopy kind of guy — and seeing the two sit together made Crump look like Bozo's next meal.

The chihuahua, named Squirt, looked exactly like Ren from *Ren & Stimpy*. Squirt licked my hand for the duration of the drive until it was completely shellacked with chihuahua slobber.

The guy who drove the truck was named Steve. As we drove through town, someone on every street corner waved at him and yelled "Howdy, Steve!" like in a beer commercial. I guess Steve had towed all of these people at one time or another, and they wanted to stay on his good side in case they got in a jam.

Steve asked a lot about the band, and offered a few "Oh-I-was-once-young-and-rebellious-like-you-guys" anecdotes, which we got often. He said years ago he had "long hair like Willie Nelson, but decided to cut it off because middle age was creeping up." What a rebel.

I asked Steve how he liked Walterboro, trying to size up the place in case we had to stay longer.

"Oh, we have no problems here," he said in a disturbing sort of monotone. Bad answer.

We pulled into TC Import Repair Shop, owned by the legendary Tammy, a hulking Valkyrie of a woman, whose first order of business was to remove the engine from the rest of the van. In medical terms, this would be the equivalent of open-heart surgery, the difference being that a doctor would remove the heart from the body and carefully place it in an incubator while continuing the operation. Tammy just sort of let the engine fall to the floor and didn't worry too much about the nuts and bolts rolling loose on the ground. Wyatt was almost in tears.

With little to do, the rest of us poked around Tammy's shop, checking out her tools in the garage and the heaps of rusty auto parts in the back. Beneath the hot South Carolina sun, we were getting tense and began speaking curtly to each other, as the situation was turning disastrous.

Then I saw an electrical outlet and had an idea. Before I could think it through, I blurted:

"Hey, let's plug in and play!"

Scott and Chuck just looked at me.

"Aw, c'mon! It'll be fun!"

At that moment I felt like the entire Brady Bunch rolled into one annoying ball of sunshine. But Chuck conceded there wasn't anything better to do, and Scott begrudgingly agreed. So we set up amid the rusted VW carcasses outside Tammy's garage, my amps sitting atop a thicket of weeds growing out of the cracks in the concrete.

With no P.A., the vocals were only as loud as we could shout them, and, being outdoors, the sound was weak. But as we dorked out and slammed around with Bill and Wyatt, our glum demeanor instantly rose. We gestured to drivers on the road in front of Tammy's shop, playing our guitars between our legs Spinal Tap-style and tongues extended, no doubt convincing them great things were in store for Walterboro now that Spoke was in town.

A few locals sauntered up to hear us play, most of whom were fascinated with Chuck, including an older gentleman who spoke to us in an exceedingly respectful manner.

"Son, I see you're sweating up a storm behind them drums," he said, "and these other guys, well, they're good and all, but you gotta *keep the beat...*" He said this as if it were a matter of global importance.

This guy turned out to be the former deputy sheriff of Walterboro, as well as, in his words to Chuck, "a drummer like yourself, only of the jazz variety." He fetched some photos of himself playing a $3,200 Ludwig set with a big band in Charleston, and reminisced about concerts he'd seen with Basie, Ellington, Armstrong and other greats. Until meeting him, I was under the impression that all old Southern cops were closet KKK members who loathed the Negro Devil Music. As usual, I was wrong.

Another enthusiastic member of the cozy gathering of onlookers was a fellow named Abe. Abe is the kind of guy you always see hitchhiking but never getting a ride. Dressed in classic "stranded and luckless" attire (soiled jeans, ripped muscle shirt, worn cowboy boots, army cap, missing teeth), Abe seemed genuinely thrilled when I let him play my guitar, where he banged out creaky renditions of "La Bamba" and "Smoke on the Water." He would later offer us chili. I liked Abe.

As we continued to play and the afternoon wore on, Tammy called a DJ friend who worked at a local adult-contemporary/country radio station. She told him we were a "big rock band" from out of town and convinced him to put us on the air. To our disbelief, he wanted to interview us "and play a song or two."

Priscilla, a friend of Tammy's, drove me and Scott to the station (called WONO, as in "Whoa no!") while Chuck guarded the equipment at the garage. Though Priscilla was as truly kind-hearted as anyone I've ever met, a leisurely stint in a padded cell might do her wonders. A self-proclaimed "Jewish-American princess turned chicken farmer," poor Priscilla looked as if she'd been dragged behind a four-by-four through the Blue Ridge Mountains for the last decade. She bore weighty, bloodshot eyes behind a near-emaciated face, and sometimes her run-on conversations seemed to border insanity:

"Last-night-my-two-little-monsters-my-little-boys-I-mean-I'm-always-calling-them-monsters-they-was-creeping-under-the-house-looking-for-some-brass-knuckles-my-older-son-found-and-I-had-to-go-after-them-under-the-house-because-a-few-months-ago-one-got-stuck-with-his-head-pinned-underneath-one-of-them-beams-along-the-stacks-of-cinder-blocks-we-use-for-a-foundation-and-I-gave-him-a-whooping-when-I-finally-got-him-unstuck-because-there-ain't-nothing-under-there-but-poison-snakes-which-I-know-because-this-one-time-I-saw-my-uncle-get-bit-behind-the-knee-by-a-poison-snake-when-he-was-under-the-house-fixing-the-plumbing-or-something-and-he-made-a-face-I-will-never-forget-to-this-day-a-face-like-THIS..."

Added to her excitable personality, Priscilla drove like a blind chimp on crank at the Indy 500. I would've been more relaxed on a derailing rollercoaster. I clutched the dashboard for the whole drive, my knuckles white. When we eventually arrived at WONO, Scott and I got out of the car in a cold sweat.

Oh yeah: during the drive, Priscilla said how happy she was that some *real* culture had come to Walterboro.

Real culture — she meant us. Spoke.

Ha!

Inside, we were introduced to Mark the DJ, an affable guy with a great on-air personality even if he was a little clumsy in the brains department (he screwed up the radio program twice — including 45 seconds of dead air — in the relatively short time we were there). But Mark's informal attitude relaxed us immediately. "Hey, we'll just gab on the air," he said. "Y'know, real loose-like."

Though irresistibly friendly, Mark struck me as the sort of person who would tell you his life story while waiting in line to pay a traffic fine. Pity the poor bartender who hears all of Mark's woes.

Mark could deduce from our appearance that Spoke was not going to fit the program director's pansy-ass format, so he slotted us between the Little River Band and Garth Brooks and gave a precautionary message to listeners: "Okay, y'all, we're, uh, gonna play something a little different, so, y'know, keep an open mind and, uh, turn the volume on your radio down a little, ha, *but don't touch that dial...*"

While Chuck's song "Just a Thought" — our poppiest and most radio-friendly, sort of — played over the mighty Walterboro airwaves, Mark was worried that his anal-retentive boss would call and bitch about us. But the only call was from a guy asking if we were "wearing flip-flops and had peace signs on [our] foreheads," whatever that meant.

We plugged Tammy's shop incessantly until some executive honcho gave us the word to scram. Before we left, Mark assured us a gig at a bar in town if we weren't moving by nightfall, but warned us it was a little "raw." I pictured a miniature version of Gilley's with a mechanical bull in the middle and local cowpokes throwing spent Coors bottles at us: *"Hey, you fay-guts gonna play some Sex Pees-tuhls? Har har..."*

Still, everyone had been so accommodating and hospitable in Walterboro that we considered the possibility. We thanked Mark for the fun at WONO and returned to Tammy's, where we were greeted by a bazillion little kids running amok, who:

- just got home from school.
- just escaped from a zoo.
- just walked off death row.

These kids overtook Tammy's lot like child-sized locusts, destroying everything in their path. To my left, I watched as a group of kids took a dead bird and repeatedly slammed its little corpse against a dumpster. To my right, I saw another group aiming BB guns at anyone within a 30-foot radius. In front of me, children were dragging other children into traffic. Behind me, kids were throwing paper airplanes — a seemingly harmless activity, except all of the paper airplanes were crashing into *my* head.

And every kid there wanted to play Chuck's drums: "Hey man, where them sticks?" Chuck frantically hid his kit away, lest The Brood beat it to oblivion. One of these demon-tykes, maybe nine years old, bashed the hell out of a phone in Tammy's office with a big hammer when I told him he couldn't have four pieces of our pizza to give to his thieving gang. I thought he was going to kill me.

Look, I adore kids, truly. But a big pitcher of Kool-Aid laced with a quart of horse tranquilizer would have come in mighty handy right then. I worry for Walterboro's future.

While all of this was going on, Tammy was finishing her repairs on the engine. When it was time to fit it back into the chassis, we were so anxious to go that Scott and Wyatt jumped under the van to help screw the thing in.

With much elation, we loaded ourselves and our equipment back into the van. With great generosity, Priscilla and Tammy gave us a bunch of peanut-butter sandwiches (which we never expected to eat) and a foot-tall jar of mint tea for our travels. Wyatt turned the ignition, the motor roared and everyone applauded. It sounded as good as a VW bus ever would. As we pulled out of Tammy's shop, 20 Walterboroers were waving, jumping and blowing kisses at us. We actually found ourselves sorry to leave.

As we veered onto the highway and the sun set into darkness, I fell asleep with the good people of Walterboro on my mind, lulled to dream by a Billie Holiday/Bad Brains mix tape playing on my Walkman. We were rolling again, with our show waiting for us in Wilmington later that night. Finally, all was well.

For an hour.

Catastrophic events were unfolding. We were losing electricity. The van's lights were dimming. The alternator was dying a slow, tortuous death. Eventually we coasted to the side of the interstate, more than 75 miles north of Walterboro. All power was gone.

"Wyatt," I said, "your van sucks."

We found a small halogen lamp in Wyatt's emergency kit, the only light source available to us on the nighttime road. With no other food, we relished those slimy peanut-butter sandwiches and that jar of luke-warm mint tea, even if it did taste like a bucket of backwash with chewed wads of Wrigley's Spearmint marinating at the bottom. We unanimously decided to stay together rather than split up and find help, figuring that the five of us were better off pushing the van together than one of us lying in a roadside ditch with a slit throat. Plus, how far could the next populated exit be?

So we pushed. And pushed. And pushed.

For six miles.

In the rain. In the dark. Nudging a two-thousand pound VW bus inch by inch on the side of the road, within spitting distance from flashing, roaring 18-wheeler trucks tearing down the highway at 80 miles per hour, nearly pegging us from behind in a bloody nanosecond.

Six fucking miles.

We leaned our weight against our forearms on the back of the van, our hands clasped on its blue steel body in an unintentional prayer position. We were soaked from the drizzle and by our own sweat. The halogen lamp, which we duct-taped to the van's rear window as a hazard light, bathed us in a dreamy, faded blue glow. Everything was wet, dark and weakly illuminated in cyan.

Hours passed. Everything came in flashes. Fireflies in the forest on the right; the flood of noise, speed and searing white headlights on the left. When there was no traffic, nothing could be heard but the gentle rain hitting the roof of the van, our sneakers squishing beneath us with each step, and the five of us breathing hard.

After three hours, a policeman drove up.

"Y'all need a tow truck?" he asked.

None of us had enough money.

"Y'all have Triple A?"

Nope.

"Hmm. Tough break. Keep pushing then. Good luck."

Six fucking miles.

After five hours, we found an exit. Heaving the van up the off-ramp, I thought I'd tear every muscle battling the road's incline. On the verge of throwing up, I'd never before considered gravity such a formidable enemy.

We rolled the van from the off-ramp into the parking lot of a cheap motel and packed into a single room. We bought beef jerky sticks and potato chips and ice cream at a 24-hour convenience store across the street, then lounged deliriously, too tired to sleep, too dazed to fully comprehend what we had done. Wyatt fell into one of his 10-minute laughing fits, where the veins pop up in his shaved head and his stomach aches from laughing too hard.

"I thought this would be a vacation," he said. "This is hell!"

We had exhausted ourselves stupid. It was almost dawn. We had yet to play a show. I fell asleep in a stiff wood chair and it felt like a cloud.

After four hours of sleep, Wyatt tracked down a mechanic named Lilton, a Pillsbury doughboy in overalls — bald, plump, happy. He took the alternator home for repair while we ate lunch at a nearby Baptist-food buffet.

The eats sucked. Everything was bland and fried mercilessly to ensure all nutritive value had been eliminated. Wyatt grossed out everyone by eating "ambrosia salad," that terrifying pink glop that I'm pretty sure was used for the evisceration scenes in *Re-Animator*. As I wolfed down a plate of popcorn shrimp, averting my eyes from the atrocity on Wyatt's plate, I overheard the group sitting behind me talking about "being saved by the Lord."

From what I could hear, the young fellow at the head of the table was recounting his "aural (oral?) experience with Jesus" to his fiancée's family, who interrupted his story with "amen" and "praise the Lord" every 10 seconds. "I want to start a ministry so everyone will feel Jesus like I have," he said.

When I turned around to take a gander at the guy, I was shocked to behold a petite Rod Stewart-lookalike of a man with thin, prissy lips and a neatly feathered coiffure, like a fresh graduate from a beauty school. He was a far cry from the old Jerry Falwell or Billy Graham archetype. The South is indeed changing.

Returning to meet Lilton at the van, I met a blond, world-weary ex-hippie named Jim sitting at a table in the gas station's adjoining "caffay." Jim apparently supervised the construction of electrical units at a prison being built less than a mile away. Before that, he said he sold LSD for a living, almost 10 years. He claimed he imported the acid in crystal form from "amateur chemists" in Switzerland and California, then liquefied it and sold it to kids who were making blotter sheets.

I asked him if he found it ironic that he was building a place where people would be incarcerated for similar pursuits. "Not really," he said.

Jim told me a few drops of LSD concentrate absorbed through the skin can send a person tripping harder "than a moth in a bag of model glue." He spoke eloquently of the physiological effects of acid, as well as its chemical make-up and the economic and legal logistics of the stuff. By the end of our conversation, I felt I knew more about acid than the average DEA agent.

He also told some grisly accounts of electrocutions he'd seen working as an electrician. "Sometimes you can see the skin charring," he said. Since Lilton was installing the fixed alternator and I was starting to feel squeamish, I said goodbye to Jim.

Lilton finished under the hood. He had a smile on his face from the moment we met him, but when we paid him what little money we had left, that smile got a hell of a lot bigger.

As we motored onto the highway with the restored alternator powering the VW bus, we were all pretty nervous. What toil awaited us? What twisted fate was in store for us next? With each passing mile, however, our anxiety eased a little, until it seemed clear that we were finally leaving the Walterboro saga behind. With a weary, collective hope in a semi-crippled van, we blazed our way north to resume our shambles of a tour. Over the next few nights, we played some shows in the Carolinas and had a good time, and would later return home without a hitch — none of which was as memorable (or fun, really) as those first crazy nights.

Since then, I haven't set foot in another Deadhead mobile — nor the otherwise fine town of Walterboro, S.C.

tommy

A record producer really gets paid for how much he suffers.

GABE PAUL (PARAPHRASED)

If you ever hear one of our records and think it sucks, don't blame Tommy Hamilton. He tried.

Tommy, founder and proprietor of Georgia Street Recording Studios in Tallahassee, produced all of our records. He was truly a "producer" — not a "mixer," "recorder" or "engineer" — in that he assisted us in every aspect of the recording process, massaging the songs into something reasonably listenable, advising us on mixing arrangements, keeping us in time with the proper tempo sequences, and all but slapping our backs to burp us. Fronting a fantastic punk unit of his own — a Hüsker Dü-cum-Die Kruezen three-piece called Gruel — Tommy had a great ear for raw, powerful underground rock, and he let bands experiment freely even when a good result seemed unlikely, a willingness most producers and engineers are too domineering to possess. The fact he only charged $15 an hour didn't hurt, either.

Besides entertaining us with war stories of recording mind-crushingly boring metal bands ("All day, they kept wanting me to tell them their music was 'killer shit.' They kept saying, 'Ay man, thet thar's some *kee-ler shee-yut*, ain't it? Some *kee-ler shee-yut...*'"), Tommy had a fine video collection, which included Herschell Gordon Lewis' classics "Blood Feast" (1963) and "2,000 Maniacs" (1964), early Black Sabbath concept videos, a Traci Lords bootleg and a fantastic documentary on tornados. His coffee table was the dumping grounds for a library of scary grindcore fanzines from Sweden, Brazil, Malaysia and other improbable places. Going to Tommy's was like spending a weekend at your cool older brother's pad at college.

Tommy's studio was arranged all over his house, with the mixing board, DAT machine, 8-track recorder, monitors and effects racks in his bedroom. This meant we would stink up Tommy's most intimate living quarters while listening to the same songs drone on for hours — sometimes days — during mix-down. For every session, he whole-heartedly opened his home to us, and we returned this gratitude by not showering for our entire stay.

Recording started by nailing down the drum track. Tommy would strategically place his microphones around Chuck's drums and record him while we played in the background, providing the foundation for each song. The remaining time would be spent building separate guitar, bass and vocal tracks over the rhythm. Because thick, multi-layered guitars were the cool thing to do at the time, I sometimes stacked four or five tracks of guitars on top of each other for a deep, rich, wall-of-noise effect. We'd also do stereophonic duo-vocal tracks to beef up the voice in the mix. This kind of "cheating" is frowned upon by recording purists — and rightly so — but it did improve our sound, which needed all of the improvement it could get.

Recording vocals was hell for me. By the last song of each session, my voice would be so cracked and strained I'd all but spit up pieces of larynx. I was perpetually off-key, quavering, awful. This didn't bother me so much in concert, but for the permanent documentation of our music I wanted my vocals at their best. Sucking bagfuls of mentholated lozenges and drinking glass after glass of plain hot water, I'd stand in front of the microphone in the hot, tiny recording room next to Tommy's bedroom, screaming my lungs out for hours.

"Don't worry about it," Tommy would say. "You're your own worst critic. I think your voice sounds good. It sounds *you*."

Good ol' Tommy.

By the time we recorded our third 7-inch, we had grown so close to Tommy that we decided to crank-call him. Scott, a master cranker, phoned him one afternoon with a bogus recording solicitation.

"Howdy Tommy, I'm Hank," Scott said in his best fake Alabama backwoods drawl. "We're in this metal band and we wanna record at your studio 'cause we hear you're the best."

"Okay," Tommy said, mellow as ever. "Which band did you say you were in?"

"That ain't important. We're metal. You like metal, right?"

"Well..." Tommy was hesitant to admit it to strangers, but he *loved* metal, even bad metal, like this horrible Morbid Angel tape we brought him once. He went nuts over it.

"Yeah, metal's fine."

"All right then," Scott said. "We're gonna come down there and record with you at... lessee now... tomorrow."

"Tomorrow?"

"Yup. Bright and early. We'll be there around, oh... 6 a.m."

"No, wait — you're telling me you'll be here *tomorrow*?"

"That's right. And lemme tell ya somethin', Tommy, you ain't never heard nobody like us. We're some kick-ass metal. You ever heard of Megadeth? *We kick Megadeth's ass.* That's why we're recording with you because we hear you're the best."

"Look, man, you can't come tomorrow."

"That's all right. That's no problem. We'll get there early."

"No, I'm saying I'm all booked up tomorrow. I'm all booked up for the next two months. We'll have to reserve some time in March or something, but I absolutely cannot do it tomorrow."

"That's okay. Tomorrow's fine with us."

"Another band's recording here! I can't record your band because I already have people who've reserved time!"

"Are you saying these people are better than us? 'Cause you could get yourself in a shitload of trouble saying something like that, buddy."

"Oh, Jesus... Look, I'm *telling* you, if you want to record here you've got to reserve some time in the future."

"Okay. I see your point. We'll do that. Say, how much you charge anyway?"

"Fifteen bucks an hour, plus the 8-track and DAT."

"But you'll lower it for us 'cause we're so kick-ass, right?"

Tommy chuckled. "Who are you guys again?"

Scott ignored the question and continued. "Okay, so we'll book some time with you and you'll make us a great demo, one that'll, y'know, get us a deal with a big record company or something, right?"

"Uh, right." By now anyone but Tommy, ever the testament to human tolerance, would've hung up.

"Now," Scott said, "I gotta tell you something. We got this problem. Well, it ain't exactly a problem..."

"Uh-huh," Tommy said.

"It's our drummer."

"Okay..."

"And whenever we record he gets really drunk."

"Okay..."

"I mean *fucked up*."

"Okay..."

"'Cause he can't play good if he ain't wasted. Problem is..."

"What?"

"Well, he gets in fights when he's drunk."

"Fights," Tommy repeated stoically.

"Yeah," Scott said. "Usually with the producer."

You could almost hear that last straw break Tommy's back.

"With the producer," Tommy said.

"Uh-huh. One time we tried to record with this other guy and our drummer up and beat the shit out of him."

"Right..."

"Put him in the hospital and that was the end of that. That's why we came to you."

"Me?"

"We figured since you're the best and all, you could handle somethin' like that. Can you believe it, our drummer smashed the guy's head right into his own mixin' board. Ain't that some shit!"

"Okay, look..." Finally, we pushed the imperturbable Tommy Hamilton over the edge. "I am not recording you tomorrow — *period*. And if there's any threat of violence, I won't record you at all."

"Don't worry," Scott said. "I bet we can hold him back."

"I don't even want to *think* of the possibility of that happening. My studio is my home, and—"

"A man's home is his castle. No arguin' with that."

"Yeah. Exactly. Y'know, this sounds pretty weird. Maybe you should—"

"Look, we'll just keep our drummer away from you."

"Man, I don't even think—"

"You don't think what?"

"Maybe it's not such a good idea—"

"Hey, our drummer's sitting right here and he's getting the idea you don't want to record with him."

"Not if he's gonna try to kill me!"

"Well he says he don't appreciate that kinda shit-talking."

"Shit-talking?"

"He says maybe you and him wanna fight *now*."

"No! No! Listen—"

"All right then," Scott said. "We'll be there bright and early tomorrow morning, so get ready — *and don't worry about a thing*."

"WHAT THE FU—"

(*Click.*)

A few weeks later, we revealed to Tommy that we were the ones who perpetrated the hoax, to his relief. He thought it was pretty funny, but he was concerned that it might have been his fiance's ex-boyfriend, who, coincidentally, was making similar threats against him at the time.

Still, in typical Tommy fashion, he wasn't too uptight about it.

"The scary part is, you guys don't know how real that was," he said. "I get calls like that from bands a couple times a month, and you just have to sit there and humor them because in their minds they're the next Nirvana. And you never know — maybe they are."

A hell of a guy, that Tommy Hamilton.

drugs

We are all born mad. Some remain so.

SAMUEL BECKETT

Call me bull-headed. Call me unenlightened. But I think the age-old affiliation between drugs and rock'n'roll is a culturally exalted load of horseshit. I don't care what "genius" wrote which "masterpiece" under the influence of a cocktail of substances that would, in most instances, paralyze an elephant. The sonic muse isn't found in the bong, bottle or syringe — at least not for me.

My choice to shun drugs is, of course, my own affair, and I go to great lengths not to impose it on anybody who chooses otherwise (meaning 98 percent of my friends), nor could I give two fucks as to how uncool my sobriety might seem to anyone else. My psyche is unglued and delusional enough without baking, warping, numbing and generally aggravating it more with a bunch of chemicals best used for scouring tile countertops ("New, Improved PCP — *Better Than Soft Scrub*").

Hey, it's your choice. But if you're like me, endowed with an innate buzz that's constantly heightened by the never-ending havoc of this chaotic, fascinating world, attempting to temporarily intensify (or dull) one's consciousness only diminishes the whole trip of living. If I can't generate fun without tweaking my senses, then that, for me, is a deficiency no drug could fix.

Plus, I've got my sanity to look after. Hell, I'll admit it: I have a healthy fear of what some drugs would do to me — or, more so, what I would do under the influence of some drugs. I've met people who are very responsible and organized in spite of their drug habits, people who've gotten through law school smoking crack, people who drive commercial rigs on U.S. highways for days on crystal meth. I, however, don't share this "quality." Any drug ingestion on my part would lead to big, complicated problems — of which I have enough already, thank you very much.

Having checked out the drug scene over the years, I've come to accept all recreational substances with a pretty low regard (though the current illegality of some drugs — pot especially — seems ludicrous to me). Yet I wouldn't align myself with the current straight-edge movement, whose rabidly conformist, militant puritanism has grown so fascistic and severe. My refusal to partake in chemical usage is mine alone, and it's never kept me from raising hell.

I don't mean to sound self-righteous. If getting wasted works for you, if it's your way of enjoying life, if you're not destroying yourself or anyone else, fine. I'm glad you're having a good time.

But me — I'm fucked up just being here.

warehouse

Walls have ears.

Four times a week, we were greeted by a giant billboard lording over a dusty parking lot, commanding us to:

"*Eat* BEEF *Every Day!*"

Thus for every practice at our second warehouse — a legitimately rented space with locks on the barbed-wire gate — this billboard was a reminder that we had arrived at the threshold of death.

For cows, anyway. Our practice space was located directly across a huge cattle pen where cows were held before being moved to a slaughterhouse to become Big Macs. On most nights, you could hear the last wails of the cattle before they were carted off to the chopping block — "death moo's" we called them, existential cries of doomed bovine who most definitely did not want you to *Eat* BEEF *Every Day.*

Unfortunately, the death moo's didn't drown out the metal bands which, as with our first warehouse space, flanked our every side. These guys — women were a rarity here — were more respectful than our former metalhead neighbors, since most were older and more serious about their music. We were amazed by their discipline, how they'd repeat the same scales and solos for hours every night. The other warehouse rooms were occupied by scary tree-surgeon people, big mean guys with chainsaws and high-grade mulchers at close reach. They were always guzzling beer and giving us the evil eye.

It was all pretty creepy. Seated in an eerily quiet, semi-desolate trailer-park part of town, it was the sort of place you'd expect to find a severed head in the foliage across from the badly lit parking lot. For practicing our songs in reasonable privacy, however, it was pretty much perfect.

Splitting the $100-a-month rent, we shared the 12- by 20-foot room with some friends in a band called The Bicycle Thieves, a sensible, friendly group of guys who spun pleasing, taut pop tunes. They practiced around dinner time and we practiced after midnight, so our schedules never conflicted. It was a good arrangement.

Having a practice space to call your own, where you can leave your instruments safely and be able to experiment with new song ideas without the burden of irritating (or impressing) anyone within earshot, is essential to the development of most bands. Since warehouses were hard to find in Gainesville at the time, we felt fortunate in stumbling upon this one. It grew to be something of a sanctuary for the three of us, a place where we wouldn't be bothered or distracted.

Not that it was impenetrable. Despite locked gates, curious strangers still managed to wander right in, following the noise to its source. One lanky fellow, maybe 19, came by late one night and plopped himself on the floor as we played.

"I was walking around and heard somebody playing a Germs song," he said when we stopped playing.

We informed him it was a Spoke song.

"Never heard of 'em," he said, his eyes darting around in a manner that made us nervous. "I think they're ripping off the Germs."

Then, without our asking, he gave us all the details of his life to the present moment, ending with: "I just enlisted in the Army and I'm supposed to go to Libya after basic training. You can get to Libya in less than 10 hours these days. And I gotta get a gas mask and some kind of suntan lotion or something. It's for the poison gas, so you don't get blisters. Hey, anybody tell you guys y'all sound like the Germs?"

Months later, during a pre-show afternoon practice, a guy waltzed in while we were drilling through songs and introduced himself as "Crazy Larry." He was the archetypical, indeterminably aged vagabond, smelling like dirt and alcohol, slurring his words; the only thing missing was a crunched top hat and polka-dotted hobo bag on a pole over his shoulder. While we played our Egg Hunt-soundalike number "Crushed," he started slamming with our pal Chris Campisi and Scott's brother Andy, who were hanging out with us. The moshing threesome got a little out of control, and at the apex of the song Crazy Larry lost all equilibrium and fell head-first into our equipment.

"I'll pay for the damages!" he said, poking his scruffy head out of the pile of drums and guitar amps like a character out of *Hee-Haw*. "I swear!"

Surveying the wreckage, we found our mike cord severed, the knobs on my distortion pedal knocked off, and a drum rim bent. Crazy Larry left apologizing profusely, promising to compensate us. We never saw him again.

As expected, by the time we disbanded and left the warehouse, its original good condition had eroded in much the same manner as the

SpokeHouse. When I asked for some of our security deposit back, the manager laughed. I removed my name from the lease and we bequeathed it to some friends in other bands, who, as far as I know, did the same when they disbanded. Successive generations of Gainesville bands have now endured the death moo's, metalheads, tree surgeons and Crazy Larry's, all in the pursuit of sculpting raw noise into something beautiful. It's a heritage I hope will continue.

lyrics

Words, like nature, half reveal and half conceal the soul within.

ALFRED LORD TENNYSON

Writing lyrics is, for me, the worst part of being in a band. When faced with having the task of creating words for a new song, I'd rather gnaw off my left testicle.

This is partly because lyrics are really important to me. They give meaning and shape to constructed sound — sometimes, when crafted masterfully, an identity more powerful than the music itself. Lyrics can make a piece of music evocative, something you can attach your thoughts to, something that becomes a part of your consciousness. Given that I care a lot about my songs, I try to write the best words I can for them, usually setting impossibly high standards for myself.

The disappointing reality, however, is that lyrics — in rock-'n'roll, at least — aren't very significant at all. They're the intellectual frosting of a visceral artform. For the most part, trying to make any real lyrical statement in a rock song almost contradicts the genre. As long as a stream of syllables flows pleasantly with the music, any set of words will do. Good music sung in other languages (or, in the case of Dead Can Dance and the Cocteau Twins, nonexistent languages) isn't less enjoyable because the words aren't understood. "Louie Louie," the godfather of all three-chord trash songs, couldn't possibly be better if we could get anything more out of it than "we gotta go" and "yah yah yah." Most Top 40 songs have the dumbest words imaginable, but people still eat them up. Why? Because rock lyrics mean jackshit.

I guess it depends on who's doing the writing. Some people seemed born to put words to music. People like Shane MacGowan, whose brain has supposedly been marinating in lager for the better part of two decades, whose decrepit teeth would make a family dentist leap from his office window in horror. MacGowan crooned, yowled and spat for Irish hellions The Pogues, describing scenes and characters worthy of Charles Dickens.

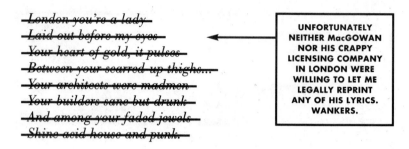

~~London you're a lady~~
~~Laid out before my eyes~~
~~Your heart of gold, it pulses~~
~~Between your scarred up thighs...~~
~~Your architects were madmen~~
~~Your builders sane but drunk~~
~~And among your faded jewels~~
~~Shine acid house and punk.~~

UNFORTUNATELY NEITHER MacGOWAN NOR HIS CRAPPY LICENSING COMPANY IN LONDON WERE WILLING TO LET ME LEGALLY REPRINT ANY OF HIS LYRICS. WANKERS.

Or Billy Bragg, who, in his thick Cockney way, brilliantly injects uncommon bite, verve and soul into even the most mundane subjects.

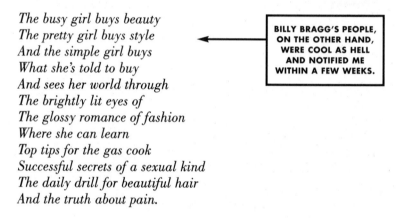

The busy girl buys beauty
The pretty girl buys style
And the simple girl buys
What she's told to buy
And sees her world through
The brightly lit eyes of
The glossy romance of fashion
Where she can learn
Top tips for the gas cook
Successful secrets of a sexual kind
The daily drill for beautiful hair
And the truth about pain.

BILLY BRAGG'S PEOPLE, ON THE OTHER HAND, WERE COOL AS HELL AND NOTIFIED ME WITHIN A FEW WEEKS.

Or Fugazi's Guy Picciotto, whose lyrics in his former band, the emocore flagship Rites of Spring, can transform me into a blubbering sap faster than you can say "over-sensitive."

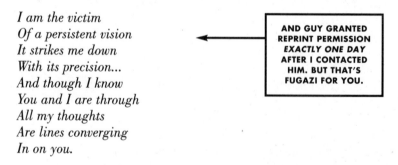

I am the victim
Of a persistent vision
It strikes me down
With its precision...
And though I know
You and I are through
All my thoughts
Are lines converging
In on you.

AND GUY GRANTED REPRINT PERMISSION *EXACTLY ONE DAY* AFTER I CONTACTED HIM. BUT THAT'S FUGAZI FOR YOU.

Or Bob Mould, Exene Cervenka, Tom Waits, Billy Childish, D. Boon, Joe Strummer, David Gedge, Q-Tip, Nick Cave, Ian Curtis — all folks who've turned their music into sonic literature.

I do not possess their gifts. I spend months — *months* — writing a mere 30 words for a song, then sulk for months afterwards about how terrible those 30 words are.

What's worse, nobody could understand what I was singing. All of my words came out sounding like I was gargling tar. My voice had the ability to take a fine verse like:

"Why can't I close my mind to this constant dictation,
It lends its direction to my every inclination..."

And muck it up into:

"Bluh bluh bluh bluh bluh bluh bluh-ation,
Bluh bluh bluh bluh bluh bluh-ation..."

And, like most lyrics, no matter how much time I spent on the words, they had no impact on anything. The political songs did nothing to change the world. The love songs never eased my heartbreak and didn't get me laid. The songs about friends who died didn't bring them back. And though a song about my allergies called "Antihistamine" didn't stop my hay fever, it was fun to play.

The only lyrics I penned that I felt had any relevance were purely by accident. "Dark City Sister" was a rather heavy-handed attempt to illustrate perpetual cycles of gender hostility through the exchange of a female prostitute and an abusive male client. It was a subject in which I had no experience, so it was essentially fictitious.

Because I hate when people quote their own lyrics, and because it's a long song, I'm only going to reprint a portion of the words:

All gospels deny
That her life is worth cherishing
She lives off men's deficiencies
To feed her, to feed off her.

Undressing his body,
He screams at her
He beats her to the floor
And the blood stains the tile
A little more,
Just a little more...

And the child she was
Is a memory half gone.
And the child she is
Passes suitably for him
To unleash upon.
And the child she had
Never breathed past
Its fourth month.
Tonight her childhood pleads:
"Good evening death
Let's come undone."
Dark City Sister.

It took me the better part of three months to complete the "Dark City Sister" lyrics. We experimented with the finished result one hot evening at our warehouse, and made our way home after midnight.

We stopped at a gas station. As we parked by a pump, a woman cut in front of Scott's car towards the pay booth, walking fast. She was petite, wore a lot of make-up and never took her eyes off the ground.

"That woman looks really insecure," Scott said, "like she's taken a lot of shit in her life." I didn't pay attention, figuring Scott was just being judgmental.

A few minutes later, after we filled the tank and were about to leave, we heard screams from the station.

"Let go!"

A man with short blond hair, wearing a white t-shirt, jeans and cowboy boots was pulling the woman by the arm.

"Help me!" she screamed to the customers standing nearby. *"Please!"*

The people around her walked off, looking in other directions.

I got out of the car. A guy on the other side of the gas pump came by us for a better look.

"Don't wanna get between a spat like that," he said. "Best not to get involved."

I looked at Scott and Chuck. None of us knew what to do.

"Don't let him take me!" she screamed at us.

The man wrapped his arm around her neck and started dragging her to a car.

I walked towards them.

"Hey pal," I said, approaching him. "Let her go."

He was expressionless. No fury, no fear, nothing.

"Everything's fine," he said with a forced calm while struggling with her. "Be on your way."

"*No!*" she cried.

"She doesn't wanna go with you," I said, trying to sound commanding as I inched closer. "Let her go."

He didn't reply. He just stared at me, holding her in a headlock, his eyes stuck to mine.

Standing less than 10 feet away from him, I felt a strange chill, a bad calm. I felt like he was going to pull a gun and put a bullet in me. That's how he looked.

"*He'll fucking kill me!*" she screamed.

He wrestled her to the car door, pushing her in from the driver's side. I hit the passenger-side window, motioning her to unlock the door.

Chuck ran to my side. Scott was behind me. She managed to roll down the car window. Chuck unlocked the door.

"I think you better leave her alone," Chuck said in a tone far more authoritative than anything I could muster.

We opened the door and Chuck climbed in the car, leveraging his body to pull her out. I was behind him, and a few other guys who joined in were behind me. We were all tugging on parts of her body.

It seemed as if the guy's grip on her would give, but he grabbed the back of her head with his right hand and slammed it forward, pinning her skull between the dashboard and windshield. He revved the car's motor and threw it in reverse.

The car door was open and I was behind it. It pushed me backwards and dragged me on the pavement. Had I not twisted out of the way, he could have run over me.

Chuck was still in the car as it pulled out onto the main street, the passenger door swinging open. He fell out, tumbling on the asphalt, just before the car sped off.

Some other guys engaged in the struggle gave chase in their car. Scott, Chuck and I watched as the red bumper lights faded down the road, vanishing into the dark.

When the police arrived, they asked us questions about the couple, the car, any clues. Nobody could remember the license plate number exactly, or the make of the car, or other pertinent information. Since we weren't seriously hurt, the cops said they couldn't really nab the guy for anything except disturbing the peace and minor assault charges, which, they said, didn't merit hunting him down.

"The world's full of abuse," one cop said to me. "Women, men, kids, everybody. But we can't charge anyone until there's a victim."

It would've been a good lyric, I thought.

But that song was already written.

zines

The whole world is a scab. The point is to pick it constructively.

PETER BEARD

Growing up, the bulk of my reading content was punk fanzines, Xeroxed and stapled and scrawled with tiny print and barely decipherable type.

It started when I was 12. On a flight from New York, where I had spent Thanksgiving with my grandparents, to my hometown of Louisville, I was sitting alone at the bulkhead of the plane, dressed in a suit and tie like a child accountant. I don't know why my family felt the need to dress me in such degrading formal-wear every time I got on an airplane; nobody else my age was so clownishly over-dressed, except at funerals. (As a result, I dress like a vagrant as an adult.)

So there I sat on the plane, looking like a little Ivan Boesky, when lo and behold who should sit next to me but Brian McMahan. At 13, Brian was the top dog of the prevailing punk rock clique at my school, and I was always trying to do things to impress him, like giving him my canned chocolate pudding during lunch on a daily basis. I figured he'd be friends with me for that.

At best, Brian *tolerated* me. I think he, like the rest of his clique, had formed the opinion that I was essentially a dull, slow-witted wanna-be. If they listened to Dead Kennedys, I'd listen to Dead Kennedys; if they got into skateboarding, I got into skateboarding; if they ate live mice, I ate live mice (thankfully, they did not). This was how I was introduced to punk — desperate social validation — and nobody can dispute that I paid my dues as a poser.

As for Brian, he'd later play guitar in Squirrel Bait and Slint, two bands of legendary status in indie-rock circles, but obviously neither of us knew that then.

So sitting on the plane in this hellaciously uncool attire next to a guy I was perpetually trying to suck up to was a moment of near-suicidal humiliation. At 15,000 feet, I wanted nothing more than to toss myself out the window. Since I was too mortified to say anything besides "Hey, Brian" and he didn't seem to want to make conversation, we sat silently looking out our windows.

Then, after about a half-hour, he said:

"You wanna check out a few zines I got in New York?"

Did I? *Hell yeah, motherfucker! Hand 'em over!*

Of course I didn't actually answer this way. I didn't even know what a zine was. But I pretended I was cool, like I'd seen plenty of zines in my world-weary 12 years.

"Yeah, sure."

Though I can't recall which titles he had — an early *Flipside*, I think — turning each page was like a rap on the head with a lead pipe. Interviews of unknown bands with sinister names (The Fuck Ups, Millions of Dead Cops, Wasted Youth), reviews of obscure and dangerous records, unashamed profanity, chaotic graphics, rude comics, anarchistic collages — all done up with a bold, autonomous, fuck-off-and-die attitude.

By the time I got to the back cover, my brain felt chewed. The freedom, fun and fury expressed in those pages were, to me, a revelation. My understanding of language, design, attitude — of communication itself — was blown open.

Of course, I didn't let on.

"Pretty cool," I said stoically as I gave the zines back. I don't think Brian noticed my trembling hand.

We touched down in Louisville and parted ways. The next day I saw him at school and gave him my chocolate pudding. Normality resumed.

After moving to Florida a few years later, I collected zines throughout high school, most of them half-assed hack jobs. Figuring my own attempt couldn't be much worse, at age 16 I threw together some rants and collages, plagiarized a fairly well-known Gary Panter print for the cover, called the collection *Oblivious Strain* and photocopied a hundred copies. It was an unqualified success: *Flipside*, *Thrasher* and *Maximum Rock'n'Roll* — the triumvirate of my reading material in those days — praised it; it got the attention of cute punk girls around town; it angered local Nazi skinheads with its anti-fascist sentiments; and it was banned from a lame Orlando record store called Murmur Records for an ad I made them: "To those who listen to the beat of a different drummer, *go beat off at Murmur...*"

Probably the best thing that came of *Oblivious Strain* was a friendship with Jen Zimmerman, the DJ of the hardcore show at WPRK (the local Rollins College radio station) and bassist/vocalist for a metalcore outfit called The Genitorturers. Jen liked the zine and interviewed me on the air about it.

"So why did you make this zine?" she asked.

"To keep people from listening to that god-awful new Cure album," I said with my best hardcore snarl, "or any Cure album, for that matter." This made sense to me in 1986.

"Ah, I see," she said. "And let me remind everyone listening that the opinions expressed by Mr. Resh do not reflect those of WPRK, Rollins College or any of its employees or affiliations."

End of interview.

Jen was a knockout. With strong, gorgeous Nordic features, bold tattoos and a cascade of dead-straight, bleached-white hair that fell to her back, she was the focus of any room she walked into, whether by admiration, arousal or shock. Her vast, all-encompassing knowledge of hardcore music somehow seemed fitting for her area of study: she attended Rollins to be a coroner. And her singing voice was anything but feminine; in one Genitorturers review, her guttural vocals were compared to John Joseph's of the Cro-Mags.

Most importantly, Jen gave me and Scott the proverbial push from the green hills of pubescence to the dark gutters of manhood. At age 17, we were a little naive as to the bizarre, ugly underbelly of the world. Jen would change that.

Being the only quality body-piercing practitioner in Orlando at the time, she showed us how one goes about piercing nipples, belly buttons and other body parts. In the late '80s, years before the piercing craze would boom among the general public, this was pretty freaky stuff, especially for two suburban greenhorns fresh from homecoming dances and multiple screenings of *Sixteen Candles*.

Another time, when Jen got a hold of two highly illegal Swedish porn tapes — one depicting Swedes fucking cows, pigs, horses, dogs, chickens and a *live* eel, another showing Swedes eating each others' shit and piss — she made a special point to invite us over.

And when her friend Mike, who worked at a hospital morgue, surprised us with a jar containing a still-born, unsplit twin fetus — man, I'll never forget that. It had one body, two heads, three arms, four legs and two vaginas; its skin was gray and wrinkled. When we walked in her room, she threw the jar at Scott without warning. I almost puked.

She laughed her head off. "You guys," she said, "I'm out to bust your cherry."

There was her S&M gear, her collection of photo books on burn victims and car crash casualties and amputees, her sick Mentors records, and her crazy friend Karen, who wanted to have sex with me so bad she made Jen announce it over the airwaves: "This next song by Agnostic Front goes out to Jon from Karen, who wants to tear your little bod apart, babe..."

The first time we met Karen was outside a warehouse show. She approached us, drunk as ever, and said, "Hey, you guys ever seen pierced nipples?" We said no, so she lifted her shirt and there they were, her boobs hanging out for public display with little silver rings in the nipples. "Whadya think?"

We had some crazy adventures with Karen, too. But as cool as she was, under no circumstances did I want to have sex with her. I wasn't too attracted to her, and by her own admission she liked really hard, animal sex (which she got plenty of, so I don't know why she lusted after a sissy like me). Plus Scott asserted that "sex with her would be like sticking your dick in a blender," which didn't sound good. And she told me her favorite song to fuck to was Black Sabbath's "Iron Man" — enough said. I'd sow my oats elsewhere.

Still, Karen persisted. "Jon," she said one night, drunk again, *"why won't you fuck me?"*

Such are the fruits of making a zine.

The Genitortures moved to L.A. for a while and signed to a major-label subsidiary. Their shtick became, predictably enough, piercing people onstage, among other "wild" sexual antics. With the theatrics as the band's focal point, I think their music's gone to shit, but I'm sure Jen isn't too concerned with what I think. She also put her medical degree to good use, working at an eye bank for which she travels to car accidents to scoop out the deceased victims' eyes. The last I heard of Karen, she was stuck in Venezuela without a passport or something.

Having left for college a year later, I befriended Var Thelin, a native Gainesvillian who published *No Idea*, an internationally distributed, full-color newsprint fanzine that contained a 7-inch record in each issue. Var's zine was well-respected, and through it he became the worldwide connection for touring punk acts to play shows in Gainesville.

I began contributing to *No Idea* around 1990. As we formed Spoke and he began with his band Bombshell, Var began moving *No Idea* toward record-label status, producing and distributing records by us, Radon, Less Than Jake and other local groups. But his determination in publishing a top-notch fanzine was hardly diminished, and fueled by his lead, by 1992 it seemed every resident of Gainesville was making a zine.

As for Spoke, the zine world granted us a great opportunity to communicate directly with creative folks whose tastes and interests were similar to our own. Since most zines were the work of solitary individuals, we were able to send our records for review by name to small publications all over the world and expect an honest critique, if and when another issue was released. Not that a zine review is all that helpful; readership is low, and it was apparent by the wild inconsistency of reviews that zine editors are not good gauges a record's quality.

For what it was worth, most of our reviews were much more complimentary than we expected, keeping our egos afloat in the stratosphere. The bad reviews, however, were a lot more entertaining, if a little off the mark:

"Uninspired, droning ... a waste of time."
"Imagine the soundtrack from a John Hughes movie meeting the current crop of 'ouch-don't-hurt-me' hardcore." (Brilliant!)
"Noisy, badly produced, headache-inducing punk."
"Too many drum rolls."
"Wimpy college rock."
"MTV-ready ... Like Pepsi you can listen to."
"Harsh, raw, unlistenable ... with songs about prostitutes."
"Unremarkable."

Interviews were even more fun, though we were terrible at them. Constantly interrupting ourselves with dumb jokes, not wanting to take ourselves too seriously "in the public eye," we were not exactly an enlightening read. The more weighty and serious the question, the stupider we got. And when our dialogue was printed or aired word for word, without the benefit of hours of careful editing, it usually sounded like three seventh-graders fist-fighting in a drunk tank.

Our interview with Pat Hughes in *Maximum Rock'n'Roll* — a publication many considered to be (for better or worse) the bible of the international hardcore/punk subculture at the time — was so intensely idiotic, it nearly ruined the whole issue. A sample:

WHAT DOES THE WORD "FREEDOM" MEAN TO YOU?
Jon: The ability for your identity to achieve growth without interference.
WE GOT MAO TSE-TUNG OVER HERE.
Jon: Who's mousy? Who's got a mousy tongue?!

Months later, in the course of touring, we met people who had seen that interview, and the opinions they expressed were always the same.

"We like your records a lot," one guy in North Carolina confided to me, "but when we read the *MRR* interview... well, we thought you were retards."

pastacore

*Everything must end.
Meanwhile we must amuse ourselves.*

VOLTAIRE

Pastacore. "Pasta" and "hardcore." That was our rallying cry.

Pastacore is eating a pound of cheap, generic-brand linguine slathered in a homemade, garlic-heavy marinara sauce, falling asleep from the pasta buzz brought on by the sudden flood of serotonin in your brain soon after, then letting the pots soak in the sink for the next week until they can be handled only with a protective biohazard suit.

It's opening a newly arrived shipment of your band's first 7-inch record.

It's accidentally pounding your fist into the jaw of a person whom you secretly have a crush on while flailing in the pit of a Wordsworth show.

It's lying on your driveway as the thermometer steadies at 90 degrees at midnight, listening to Hank Williams Sr. on a Walkman and watching the stars, wondering what music the aliens are listening to as they watch Earth.

It's treating yourself to an afternoon movie after failing a final exam.

It's starting a fake riot with your friends on a crowded street for public arousal.

It's new-wave dancing on Tuesday nights.

Pastacore is canoeing at Lake Wauburgh on weekday mornings before going to your shitty minimum-wage job, watching alligators watch you paddle away.

It's dogpiling the microphone at Radon shows, screaming the chorus of "Facial Disobedience" while pinned to the floor with five layers of bodies on top of you, then recovering from a sore ankle and laryngitis the next day.

It's skateboarding the foot-high concrete slab behind the University of Florida's department of architecture building after midnight, ollie-to-grinding its well-ground edge, then getting bitched at by the frustrated architecture students pulling all-nighters inside.

It's free pizza, burritos and sandwiches from friends employed at fast-food joints around town.

It's reading history books you found in the garbage.

It's scrubbing the mucilage of dried beer off your friend's kitchen floor from the party she had the night before without her having to ask.

It's spending your entire allotment of food money for the semester on a great amplifier, then having to eat the Hare Krishnas' free lunch at the Plaza of the Americas every day for the next three months.

It's pick-up soccer games on Saturday mornings.

Pastacore is throwing bottles against the wall of your back porch by yourself, with the fourth movement of Beethoven's Ninth Symphony blaring at full volume on your stereo until the cops arrive.

It's picking flowers for a girl you're smitten with because you're too broke to take her on a real date, then giving them to her with a compilation tape, one you recorded over Black Flag's *My War* and stayed up all night making, hoping she'll love you for it.

It's making up crazy new dances at Pat Hughes' Funkadelic Dance Parties (all old-school funk and soul, no disco) at his house with roommates Wade and Kalpesh.

It's observing the very serious girls and boys at campus protest marches fight patriarchal oppression while discreetly flirting with each other.

It's staying home and playing with your cat instead of seeing your neighbor's new band.

Pastacore is scoring a near-mint condition LP by Devo, the Germs, Chrome or Token Entry for three dollars in the Hyde & Zeke's "new used" vinyl bin.

It's watching *Cool Hand Luke* or *Meet John Doe* on Channel 51's "Starlight Theater" at 2 a.m., with half the people in the room eating microwaved nachos and the other half choking down coughs from hits of a newly purchased bong.

It's nursing the burn on the underside of your forearm from launching so many bottlerockets by hand.

It's talking politics with your hippie neighbors and having to quietly endure their unbearable patchouli stink.

It's helping a friend get through a bad acid trip, spending hours relaxing his speeding heart by playing a soothing, continuous guitar line while he occasionally pukes in the nude.

It's reclining on your living-room couch on a rainy Sunday, reading *Reid Fleming: World's Toughest Milkman* or *Eightball* comics while listening to the first Snuff album.

It's giving food to the homeless, addicted, afflicted and insane who amble through your open front door.

It's cutting, pasting and Xeroxing at Target Copy Center in the dark hours before dawn — then paying for 20 copies when you're walking out with 175.

It's cutting your 9 a.m. class to have sex.

Simply, pastacore is life lived maximally, every moment savored.

money

The superior man understands what is right.
The inferior man understands what will sell.

CONFUCIUS

I've never been too swift with economics. I have a tough enough time figuring out perplexing financial concepts like "dimes," "nickels" and "dollars," much less "short-run aggregate supply curve" or "interest-rate parity transmission mechanism." (I think that's what broke in Wyatt's van.)

The only time in my life I've ever handled money efficiently was when I was addicted to video games in the sixth grade, an obsession as beneficial to a child's blossoming understanding of finance as high-stakes baccarat. I was very thrifty then and would do anything for a quarter. I remember rescuing one from a pile of dogshit to play a game of Galaga, all too comfortable with the whore I had become.

As an adult, I've grown distrustful of money, the result of which is I never have much of it. So during Spoke's tenure, I had no intention of tangling the band in messy money affairs — an easy task, since we were usually broke.

We could do this because (with the exception of Chuck) we were in college and, though we had jobs, Scott and I were fortunate enough to be reasonably "provided for" by our parents. Here lies a big distinction: playing in a band while someone else pays your bills is easy. But playing in a band without any means of support is a far harder road, requiring band members to a). work a day job and completely dedicate what's left of their free time to the band, or b). make money off of the band, which leads to the classic ethical questions of selling out. Add variables like a wife, child and car payments, and things can get mighty complicated.

This isn't to say Scott and I had a Porsche to wreck every weekend, but we could, for the most part, eat, attend school and pay rent regularly — with the exception of the summer of 1991, when Spoke began. I wasn't taking any classes and, as was fitting, received no financial support. Unable to find a job after looking for two months, I was forced to borrow $9 from Scott for 70 packs of ramen noodles.

I ate nothing but ramen noodles three times a day for nearly a month. The hallucinations were terrible.

Since our main objective in Spoke was just to play music, we regarded any money we received as a luxury; hell, *fun* was our pay. This was very difficult for folks outside of the punk scene to understand. Because the idea of making music has become so linked with making money,* because everything associated with music is more readily seen as products and brands than art and self-expression, and because most Americans are almost religiously obsessed with material wealth, many people just couldn't comprehend the idea that we weren't doing this to generate cash. We would've done it for free. If we had to, we would've *paid* to do it.

The money a group receives for its performance, however, is a good gauge as to how much a club or promoter respects its bands, as well as an insight into a promoter's overall business ethic. If 150 kids are packed into a club to see your band at four bucks a head and you receive only $30 out of it, you're probably not dealing with credible people. Getting the money you deserve can then be, as mentioned, a tricky negotiation.

CLUB MANAGER: "Kid, 30 bucks is all I can give ya. Been a rough week for us, y'know."

Yeah, sure — but your performance just helped pay their rent. And who deserves the dough: this sleaze bag who shits on bands regularly, or you, who could put it towards more constructive ends — like buying dozens of Twinkies and tipping cows on a 24-hour sugar high?

YOU (*with fake smile*): "Well, you made a killing tonight, ha ha! C'mon, how about floating more our way?"

CLUB MANAGER: "Sorry, but that's all we can do."

YOU: "What about our guarantee?"

A guarantee is a pre-arranged price the club is willing to pay the band. But even if it's in writing, a guarantee can turn into something of a sliding scale, often sliding to the lower end.

CLUB MANAGER: "Guarantee? What guarantee? There was no guarantee."

YOU (*sheepishly*): "Oh, yeah. I was thinking of our show in Columbus. Shit."

---

* The "music as money" concept was fully realized when, in 1999, David Bowie made the future royalties of his back catalogue of songs investable on the bond market. Financial institutions reacted favorably to the unprecedented move, netting Bowie (as of this writing) an estimated $55 million, making his music — bought, sold and traded on world markets — a legitimately exchangeable commodity. *Cha-ching!*

Advanced guarantees are few and far between, and unless you're an act with a sure draw — Elvis, Sinatra, etc. — or have a very insistent booking agent, good luck getting one.

YOU (*desperate, grasping for straws*): "Look man, we came all the way from [*your town*] to play this club! We're hundreds of miles from home! We deserve some compensation!"

CLUB MANAGER (*annoyed*): "Oh, you *deserve* compensation? Maybe you'd like to be *compensated* by my associates, Rocco and Crusher. C'mere, boys..."

ROCCO and **CRUSHER**, two 400-pound neanderthals wearing "House Security" t-shirts, walk in your direction in a slow, Godzilla-like gait.

ROCCO (*baggy eyes half-open*): "Buh, yeah boss?"

CLUB MANAGER: "This kid wants some *compensation.*"

ROCCO: "Compensation?"

YOU: "Yes, I would like to know why—"

WHAM!

A purely hypothetical situation, I assure you.

Some bands split whatever "earnings" they get at the end of a night between the band members, usually ending up on several cases of Pabst Blue Ribbon. Others put the money back into the group, so all expenses — rent for the practice space, gas, fliers, food on the road, new strings and drumsticks — are paid for by the band rather than from the members' pockets.

Our band fund was kept in a plain manila envelope marked, generically enough, "BAND FUND." Sometimes it was stuffed with $10 and $20 bills; usually it was empty, save for a few loose nickels rolling around at the bottom. We scrimped and saved to keep the impact of Spoke's expenses at a minimum, and every once in a while we'd find ourselves with a cash surplus. With this we'd make T-shirts, records and other unnecessary, uninventive items with which the punk rock market is already glutted.

We especially liked cheesy novelty products. Once we tried to make Spoke matches. I created a handsome matchbook design, but the manufacturer refused to produce them because of a single line of text at the top: "*Choosy Arsonists Choose Spoke Matches.*" Go figure.

In our first record, we included the Spoke napkin. We stole a thousand napkins from a nearby Burger King, embossed "Spoke Limited Edition Napkin" on an inked hand-stamp, then proceeded to manufacture a thousand customized chin-wipers.

My last great merchandising ploy never came to fruition: Spoke after-dinner mints. Apparently there are companies who can print a word or two on peppermint hard candies with edible ink — a real miracle of progress — but I couldn't locate them.

Sometimes the money we "earned" was put to more socially conscious uses by playing benefit concerts. We loved benefits, and raised money for student unions, AIDS prevention organizations and campus political groups, sometimes several hundreds of dollars. We, of course, played for free, and the venue would sometimes take a small cut for expenses.

Often the benefit money was spent well, with noticeable results. Other times, however, the money went to some shadowy reserve, like "reimbursing personal accounts of high-ranking group officials for prior organizational expenses." This meant the group's head honcho was getting an undisclosed amount of cash for allegedly bringing Kool-Aid and Funyons to last month's "consciousness-raising session." We weren't too cool with this.

While visiting the Positive Force house in Washington, D.C., a few years before starting Spoke, I was inspired by benefit concerts they were staging: the admission price was $2 (for the club) and two cans of food (for a local homeless organization). This seemed like a great idea, since food is (or should be) an apolitical commodity: everybody's been hungry at least once in their life, and nobody wants to see anyone starve.

So I called Club Velvet — formerly Club Gravity, where we played our first show — to gauge their response to a concert where the admission price would be *only* the two cans. To this day Club Velvet stands as the most mismanaged club I've ever seen: no mixing boards, no liquor license, no security, no emergency exits, nobody taking money at the door, no fire inspections, no insurance and no housekeeping. The only reason I could see for the city allowing the place to stay open was that the co-owner was purportedly a cocaine narc, though not a very good one since everybody in town knew it (or assumed he was, anyway).

I explained to him that if he got a weekend liquor license — which is unheard of in Gainesville, but I figured as a narc he had connections — they wouldn't need a door price and could make a killing off the bar.

Amazingly, he accepted. I had my Saturday night.

I called St. Francis House, the most prominent homeless shelter in town, to see if they were cool with it. I spoke with a wonderful old lady who was flabbergasted by the idea.

"What? Punk bands want to do *what*?"

"We want to raise food," I said. "Five or six bands will play. We'll charge two cans of unopened food for admission, or two dollars if they don't have any cans. Then we'll give all of the food and money to your organization."

She was ecstatic. "I've never heard of such a thing! Punk bands! Lovely!"

Every band we approached was enthusiastic — after all, a chance to play on a Saturday night to a good crowd was the brass ring, free or not. A solid bill was arranged: Postage Paid, Wordsworth, Bombshell, Spoke, Radon and Grinch, all for two cans of food.

I designed a flier and gave it to some friends working at Kinko's; they photocopied 1,500 copies for free. Within a week, the town was completely wallpapered with benefit fliers (including the the exterior of Samantha Fox's tour bus; she was playing in town the same night). I wrote public service announcements for the local PBS radio station, which were read on air 10 times a day between opera arias and chamber-music pieces.

Added to this, my Dad was in town. He's a biologist at the University of California-Berkeley and is active in assisting the homeless community in Oakland. This would be his first and only opportunity to see Spoke, and the timing couldn't have been better.

Putting the benefit together wasn't too difficult in the weeks before, but by the night of the show, between organizing everything and stoking myself up to play, I was a wreck. At the club, as people began to filter in early, I couldn't think straight. Luckily, friends stepped up to take cans, collect money and check IDs at the door.

It was evident that people felt a greater satisfaction in "paying" real food for admission than cold cash, since it seemed a more direct means of alleviating the suffering in question. One unforgettable sight was a tall, lanky guy with a foot-high, green mohawk walking up the street toward the club — sporting the requisite paratrooper boots, multiple piercings, bleached Brit-punk jeans and a ripped Exploited shirt — carrying a can of lima beans in each hand.

Some brought bags, even boxes, of cans, and by the time the show started, we already acquired more food than we thought we'd get in the whole night. Storing them became a problem; they were taking up too much corner space and flooded into the bar area.

Club Velvet held about 250 patrons comfortably. By the time it was our turn to play, about 500 people were packed in, with enough cans lining the back section of the club to amply supply a Safeway. We could barely make our way through the crowd to the stage. As we rifled through a short set, the whole club seemed to spill over itself, slipping on the sweat-slicked floor. It was heaven.

The minute we finished, the owner-narc guy approached me looking distressed.

"Can you smell it?" he yelled.

"Smell what?" I said.

"Gas!"

"Huh?"

"There's a gas leak in the club!"

Jesus. While surveying the grounds — lit cigarettes were in every other hand — I envisioned a mushroom cloud, on Main Street, where Club Velvet *was*...

"Well," I said, my mind still rattled from performing, "if a couple hundred people burn to a crisp tonight, I guess we'll be two of them."

He didn't find this funny. He raced off to solve the problem, almost in tears. Later, what was mistaken for gas turned out to be the stench of raw sewage coming from the toilet. Typical.

The other bands were amazing. Bombshell threw a confetti-fest that had the crowd pulling bits of colored paper out of obscure body crevices for the next few weeks. As usual with Radon's set, the audience was literally stacked six bodies deep to sing "Wash Away" with Dave Rohm. And by the time Grinch played their last song — at almost five in the morning — 30 kids were still slamming hard, like they just awoke from a nap.

By the evening's end, we collected more than 1,800 cans and about $300 for St. Francis House. Club Velvet made more at the bar that night than during its whole history of operation *combined*. As my father and I — as well as Pat Hughes, my friends Frank Barber, Bill Allred, Travis Fristoe and others — heaved 200-pound boxes of cans into a van, the little slimeball who co-owned Club Velvet, whom I hadn't met before, was talking to the narc guy about "doing a bene-fit for the bums" every few months to pull in more cash.

"We can have the TV news here, we'll have commercials on all the radio stations, maybe even charge a few bucks," he said, wring-ing his hands. "Yeah, we'll pack 'em in."

Oh, I wanted to deck the filthy little bastard. Here we had given him the most profitable night in his club's existence, and, without recognizing the evening's contribution to anything but his private interests, he wanted *more*. There's always some greedy asshole with a profit margin in mind to ruin a good thing.

The next year, the St. Francis House was so overloaded with canned goods, they asked us to raise an item in higher demand: hygienic products. "Homeless folks who no longer want to remain homeless must have a clean appearance in order to get a job," explained the house administrator. So the price of admission changed to two new, unopened packages of health-care products — soap, toothbrushes, deodorant, tampons, shaving razors, that sort of thing.

The bill was Bombshell, Paste Eater, Less Than Jake, Don't Be One and us. By then, Club Velvet had collapsed under its own lax management, so the benefit was held at the Covered Dish. About 300 people attended. Huge dishwasher-sized boxes full of hygienic products were collected, as well as a big box of towels and more food.

After that, I was burned out. The idea caught on with well-connected show-business professionals in town who wanted to organize a huge, outdoor music benefit for the shelter — the kind where full-page ads announced the concert in the local newspaper, where families bring their kids and play frisbee with their dogs on the lawn.

Fine. I was tired.

Yet I walked away from these shows with this one solid notion often overlooked in the unrelenting American compulsion for financial gain: While cash is only as valuable as the goods it's spent on, the elimination of money for more appropriate capital is, in those instances when feasible, a more effective means of providing needed solutions.

I mean, try eating a dollar bill.

sex

I learned to play guitar to get laid.

STIV BATORS

I unclasped the back of her bra as Bauhaus' "In the Flat Fields" emanated from speakers at each corner of the dark room. She writhed slowly in my arms as I kissed the line of her jaw going from her chin to ear, then down her neck. When my forearm brushed against the cusp of her breast, the touch, though delicate and fleeting, resonated through my body electrically.

She was 18. I *think* she was 18. I didn't know her too well. I wasn't even all that fond of her. She and her friends would sometimes come into town for our shows. They would drink too much cheap wine and enjoy the attention of guys — namely, us — taking care of them when they were too wasted to perform such complex functions as holding a cigarette or peeing alone. Much of their conversation was filled with weird jokes, facetious snaps and dull insults, so they were actually kind of annoying.

But attractive. They were hot in a frenetic, disarrayed way. I couldn't deny it.

As we played out more, they appeared at the SpokeHouse doorstep with greater frequency, acting more flirty and groupie-like with each visit. After a particularly good show, I got it in my head that having sex with one of them would be a good idea.

"She's a sweet girl," I rationalized, a pig in heat.

So she and I were alone at the house late that evening discussing something dumb, and I started getting that anxious ache in my stomach, the ever-trusty barometer that the time was right to move. So I whipped out the most seductive line I could muster...

"Wanna go in my room and listen to some records?"

...And she said yes. I whisked her in. As I put my arms around her and gently kissed the back of her neck, she seemed pleased. A little drunk, but pleased. She made motions to proceed.

So this was what it was all about, eh? This was why rock'n'roll started and why everyone's wanted to be a rock star ever since:

for the fucking. Okay, fine.

The first half of the Bauhaus tape wasn't finished before we were rolling around naked on my bed, and I said:

"I should get a condom."

"Yeah."

While I was thoroughly enjoying every inch of her, she seemed noticeably distracted, squirming and twisting in a strange way. I didn't know if she was too drunk to derive any pleasure from me, or if she was too inexperienced to express herself sexually, or if she felt awkward with me, or if I was being an unstimulating bore — or, worst of all, if for some reason she felt forced to go through with it.

In any case, it made me uncomfortable. I don't like having sex with someone who isn't having as much fun as I am. Reciprocation is, after all, the point of it.

"Is everything okay?" I asked.

"Yeah."

"You sure?"

"Yeah."

But her body language demonstrated otherwise, and I found myself getting exasperated, even feeling sorry for her — sentiments not exactly conducive to fornication. So I did something to end it, something that not only betrayed the both of us, but (some would assert) betrayed the entire male gender, perhaps the human species itself.

I faked an orgasm.

It was dark, I was covered with a condom, and she had no way of knowing otherwise. I just made a lot of noise and shook my body and pretended I was rocked from here to Tupelo, then pulled out and threw the condom away. Heck, if any number of ex-girlfriends could do it, so could I.

She seemed relieved.

We went to sleep. Not in each others' arms, not spooning and smiling and whispering afterwards. We turned our naked backs to each other and slept alone in the same bed.

Which sucked. Call me a sissy but post-coital cuddling is what I'm all about. Blowing my wad into a bunch of female piping is not, for me, the zenith of sex. The shared, euphoric afterglow — shit, that's what I *live* for.

Awakening that morning, I opened my eyes and was startled to find the young woman in my bed. The fact that I had just porked a drunk girl whose precise age and last name I didn't know — *whom I faked an orgasm for* — was so insignificant to me, it slipped my mind.

"I'll be at the next show," she said, putting her shirt on as I still laid

in bed, my head sunk in the pillow. "When is that? Three weeks?"
I looked up at her, my shame deepening.

"Uh, something like that," I said smiling, though not a real smile.
"I'll see you then."

"Okay."

She chose not to be there. From then on, we managed to avoid
each other.

In any other era, that would have probably been the end of it, with
nothing remaining but silent, best-left-forgotten guilt. But about a
week later, as I stripped my bed for laundry, I noticed maroon stains
smeared all over the far end of my sheets, the side I didn't sleep on.

Maroon stains.

Dried blood.

Her.

My stomach sank. I thought back to our night together. I didn't
notice any blood. I knew she wasn't having her period; I went down
on her and when you do that you know *quick*. Although I wore a condom, contact with that much blood, especially during unprotected
oral sex, would surely increase the risk of contracting any number
of sexually transmitted diseases, not the least of which was HIV.
And if she was infected, she probably wouldn't know it. In any case,
she still had sex with me...

Shit.

This wasn't the first time I confronted exposure to HIV. I had been
tested a few years before because, in my last year of high school, I was
a little reckless with a woman who (I would later learn) had unprotected sex with many partners, some of whom fell into "high-risk"
categories. Feeling uneasy about it, I decided to get myself checked.

The HIV testing procedure and the waiting period afterwards were
nerve-racking enough to nearly scare me into celibacy. During
the two weeks between the blood-letting and the disclosure of the
test results, I went through hell, worrying over the outcome if the
test returned positive. As it happened, I never had to address that
possibility: the test showed I didn't have the virus.*

Now here I was a few years later in the same situation. I tried con-
tacting the girl to ask a few crucial questions about her background
and health — and exactly how she came to bleed on my bed — but
I couldn't locate her. I consulted some friends who worked at a local

---

* In this, however, lies a horrible, tragic irony that will remain with me always. Though neither
she nor I were HIV-positive, this former girlfriend, with whom I shared an intense but short and
rocky relationship, was murdered a few years later. During a routine walk in her neighborhood,
she was apprehended and stabbed multiple times. Her body was found in a ditch. She was 23.

women's clinic. Their consensus: she was either menstruating, spot bleeding from intercourse (possibly facilitated by her guzzling a six-pack earlier in the evening), or a virgin.

It sounds callous, but I was obviously pulling for her virginity. If she never had sex before, her chances of carrying HIV — or most any other disease transmitted sexually — would be greatly reduced.

So I dragged my sorry ass to the Alachua County Public Health Unit once again. Since I knew what to expect, the whole experience wasn't so dramatic. After the half-hour of questioning about the number of sex partners I'd had and lots of other clinical data, the counselor told me the odds were on my side compared to other cases, but said the HIV is a sneaky bastard, capable of rearing its deadly head in anyone having polygamous, unprotected sex.

Just desserts for trying to be a fucking rock star.

I returned two weeks later and sat in the Health Unit's waiting room, looking at the many other "clients" seated with me, wondering if they were there for the same reason. I, as well as most people my age, had never known sex without the risk of AIDS; the disease existed before I was sexually active. Does an entire generation associate sex with death in some capacity as a result? What sort of toll does that take on collective ideas about love, intimacy and gender among my peers?

While pondering these issues, a counselor called me into his office. He sat me down and asked how I was doing.

"All right," I said.

He wasted no time, looking over my paperwork stoically.

"You're..."

This is it, I thought.

Why am I here?

Why must I face this terrible shit? Why must anyone?

What if he tells me I'm going to die?

"...negative."

I exhaled.

Negative.

I walked away from the Alachua County Public Health Unit feeling once again like I got out lucky. I was relieved but bolstered.

As for the young woman, I saw her a few years later. She didn't act very friendly to me, which seemed understandable. She knew nothing of what I went through, and I chose not to bring up the issue.

From a mutual friend, I would later learn she was, indeed, a virgin. I was her first.

bigtime

Only sick music makes money today.

FREDERICH NIETZSCHE

The letter came with an electric bill, a Publisher's Clearinghouse Sweepstakes package and a public-service postcard with the picture of a missing child. It was on a weekday afternoon sometime in the spring of 1992, and I was making a peanut-butter-and-jelly sandwich when I checked the mail.

The return address was MCA Entertainment. It was post-marked "New York City." Inside, below the MCA corporate letterhead, it read:

Dear members of Spoke,

I read a review of your band in Maximum Rock'N'Roll *and am interested in hearing your material. Please send me the "Seratonin" record, or information as to how I could purchase the record.*

It was signed by an A&R rep named Stacy, who I immediately pictured as a hip young scout sporting $200 NaNa shoes from Eighth Street in Greenwich Village, probably the kind of person who eats sushi four times a week and has never heard a Creedence Clearwater Revival song in her life. I tried to imagine Stacy hunting through the smudgy newsprint of *MRR* and its anarchistic contents in her pristine New York City office, no doubt plastered with lame rock posters, before stumbling upon our review.

What piqued her interest? Was it the part of the review that said "bad production" or "mediocre emo"?

And why, despite zero effort in trying to attract any major label attention, had we already received similar inquiries from Sony, Roadrunner and Elektra Records, all requesting "material"?

We had no mainstream market potential whatsoever. For them to be scoping out us — and surely hundreds like us — something was definitely amiss.

While pondering this on the SpokeHouse porch, I was struck with a vision of things to come, a premonition of unsettling consequence. I saw friends and acquaintances to whom we once offered pasta, a floor to sleep on, hours of chatter and a place to play, now performing on late-night talk shows, selling out huge venues, grinning on the covers of self-important rock magazines and hamming it up on MTV interviews.

I saw music I'd long considered brash, challenging and even subversive used to sell cars, sneakers and other products in TV ads.

I saw newsstand magazines publishing articles on the "essential" punk records every self-respecting rock connoisseur should own, and splashy fashion spreads: "How To Look Like You've Been Punk For Years."

I saw fanzines debating what constituted "selling out" until the argument became so dull that nobody cared — and everybody did it.

I saw scholars of pop culture pontificating on punk, its history and cultural significance — and getting it all wrong.

I saw celebrities who long disavowed their punk pasts reclaim them now that it was chic, while tens of thousands of young consumers blindly mimicked an empty, appropriated "punk" pose and attitude from the images broadcast to them by a multi-billion dollar entertainment industry.

And of the hardcore contingent left behind, the pioneers and builders of this subculture whose lives were immeasurably enriched (if not shaped and saved) by punk rock back when it was still sneered at and buried low — I saw them in disarray. With the punk underground irreversibly invaded, commodified and diluted, the old guard would stand (if only momentarily) confused and divided by the freakish, unforeseen boom.

Some would ride the wave of profitability. Others would entrench themselves deeper in the underground, zealously dedicated to preserving the punk ideal, trying to keep the subculture from dissolving into a commercialized shell of itself. And others, disenchanted yet no less nonconformist, would venture to new cultural, personal and aesthetic frontiers now that punk, whitewashed in mainstream America's monocultural swamp, had become just another identity for sale at the mall.

I also saw some commotion from the next generation of restless kids. Finding punk rock pretty boring and needing to assert their own sense of rebellion, they would create a new scene — something energized, weird and unprecedented, something they could call their own, something those passé old punkers would *hate*.

Assaulted with such a jarring vision, still holding the letter from Stacy at MCA and standing on the porch, it was clear to me what had to be done.

I found a clean envelope and addressed it. I stuffed half of my peanut-butter-and-jelly sandwich in the envelope with no protective wrapping and included a letter.

Dear Stacy,

While we appreciate your interest in our band, we are declining to send our recorded material to your organization.
Instead, we're sending lunch.
Enjoy.

Love,
Spoke

The jelly was already seeping through the envelope as I dropped it in the mailbox.

**I'll be comfortable on the couch.
Famous last words.**

LENNY BRUCE

"Hey, don't get caught."

It was the dumbest thing I could've said. Scott shot a disappointed look back at me as he jumped out of the van. If he was caught, we all were. There was no point in even bringing it up.

It was after midnight. Scott and I, as well as Bill Crump and our new tour companions Ethan Duran and Anthony Sciletti, had been cruising the quiet cul-de-sacs of suburban Gainesville for half an hour, searching for a lawn gnome, yard jockey or similar piece of outdoor kitsch.

We found it.

Visible from the street, sitting in ceramic glory on an immaculately trimmed lawn, a squat, porcelain statue of a cat, about two feet tall with cartoonish features — big eyes, little ears, graceful legs that merged into its rotund body — seemed to beckon us to take it.

ABDUCT ME

Scott snatched it off the yard, ran back to the van and handed it to me. It weighed about five pounds, was hollow like a cookie jar and so fragile it would break if you looked at it too hard.

"We'll never get Fluffy back in one piece," Crump said, "Fluffy" being our newly procured statue.

"It won't break," Scott said. "Fluffy is our first priority."

This theft was not without purpose. It was done in conjunction with a tour we organized spanning the East Coast and Midwest. We were leaving the next day.

It's an old (and, at that time, unperfected) gag: everywhere we'd go, we'd snap a photo of Fluffy next to a famous monument — the Statue of Liberty, Lincoln Memorial, Niagara Falls, wherever. When we returned to Gainesville at the end of the tour, we'd write a brief first-person description on the back of each picture: "Here I am at the Statue of Liberty." Or "Thinking of you at the Lincoln Memorial." Or "Enjoying majestic Niagara Falls."

We'd then place Fluffy back in its exact location in the yard, leaving the photos and travel notes in the owners' mailbox. In a sense, our big tour was little more than an excuse to freak out total strangers. Beats blowing up cars.

Organizing this tour, our most expansive yet, wasn't easy. For months, we shmoozed with club owners on the phone, sent tapes and records to venues, coordinated dates, mapped the trail of our journey, solicited additional transportation, printed t-shirts to sell on the road, bought odds and ends for equipment, and saved enough money to cover our rent-in-absentia and travel expenses, all for a jaunt of less than a month. How some bands organize a tour spanning the better part of a year is beyond me.

Ethan talked his parents into letting us borrow their van, and Anthony agreed to follow us in his truck for a week or so, allowing us to throw in a few pieces of equipment. As it turned out, we couldn't fit all of our stuff in the van, so Anthony and his truck became permanent fixtures.

Chuck, Scott and I agreed that Ethan and Anthony would be healthy influences on the road. Ethan's quiet, low-key demeanor complimented his acerbic wit, and Anthony, a perpetual optimist, was game for just about anything. Crump, of course, was Crump: after proving his mettle in Walterboro, we wouldn't think of going on a tour without him.

Leaving Gainesville was hectic. I awoke early, knowing I had a million things to do — pack, pay bills, write notes to absent roommates, scribble last-minute phone numbers into our tour notebook, rush to finish everything. At the warehouse, I was in no mood to lift any equipment.

"Quit being crabby," Scott said to me. "I don't want this tour starting with a bad vibe."

My grumpiness was probably the result of my new "campaign of constructive restraint": with the exception of any chance encounters with willing females along the way, I vowed not to jack off for the entirety of the tour. I figured if I contained all of my manly energy, my vocals would be more raging and tortured (and thus better) by the end of the tour, when we had time slated to record an album with

Tommy Hamilton. Plus, I wanted to test my will power in case I was ever forced at gunpoint to become a monk or something.

"That's gotta be the dumbest idea I've ever heard," Anthony said. "No healthy man has ever gone a month without masturbating. You're insane."

"Anthony, your problem is you've never gone five minutes without masturbating," I said. "You should try it."

After munching down a few sticks of beef jerky — a road-trip staple, accounting for my constant heartburn — I fell asleep fast on the drive to Atlanta for our first show, quickly establishing a tour precedent: any time I'd sit in the van for more than half an hour, I'd crash. When I awoke, we were parked behind the Somber Reptile, a club located in a part of Atlanta where locals told us not to stray too far in any direction for fear of getting mugged, raped, murdered — the usual hype.

Inside, the fat manager guy seemed preoccupied with his leg, which was held in a robotic-looking, high-tech brace.

"Hey," I said, "can I get both of my amps miked?"

"Uh..." he groaned, poking around his brace. "What?"

"My amps. Can I get them miked?"

"Your amps... you want your amps *what?*"

"Miked."

No answer. This question — whether or not to put a microphone in front of the amp speakers, sending the guitar sound through the club's P.A. — was not an unusual request, given that an average of three bands probably asked him every night.

"That leg of yours," I said, pointing to the brace, "it wouldn't happen to be bionic, would it?"

"Bionic? No."

"Well, neither are my amps. Can I get them miked?"

That little wisecrack ensured they would *not* get miked.

A speedmetal band opened the show, with the singer's obligatory falsetto vocals providing us some chuckles. By the time we went on, the club was dead; a dozen 16-year-old boys, dressed exactly alike in big shorts and baseball caps bearing the names of New York straight-edge bands, stood 10 feet apart from each other, arms folded, heads bobbing uniformly in rhythm.

Some guy in the back of the room had an epileptic seizure. I only witnessed the end of it, with him convulsing on the ground and throwing up weird, otherworldly bile. I felt awful for him. Was it something we did? Did our tour openers send people into seizures?

I accidentally pulled the cord out of my guitar twice from jumping

AMPED

111

around, bringing it to an abrupt silence. This pissed Scott off, worsened by the fact that a story he told onstage fell totally flat.

"I was booking this show in North Carolina," he said, "and the guy at the club was really odd. I was pressing him for a show on this one date, and he was being all flaky about it. Finally I said, 'Look, can we get this show or not?' And he said, 'Well, there's a lot to consider, it's like all interconnected.' 'Huh?' 'Well, booking shows here is like this grand, orbital thing, and you have the moon, the stars, the meteors and the asteroids, and your band is like an unchartered comet coming out of nowhere...' What a maniac!"

The kids on the floor stared at Scott cockeyed.

"Yeah, so..." Scott's voice trailed off, "meteors, asteroids..."

You could almost hear the footsteps of people leaving.

A band called Crisis Under Control took the stage after us, playing straight forward, old-school hardcore. We were staying at their house that night in the Cambodian section of Atlanta (I was astounded that Atlanta *had* a Cambodian section), which they called the House of Hardcore. The kids living there told us how they couldn't bear listening to any music other than hardcore, and, interestingly, how much they "loved America." They said they didn't appreciate bands that advocated "anti-patriotism" (which, technically, we did at times), but they seemed to be positive, tolerant folks all the same.

Around 2 a.m., we went to Waffle House with Allen and Rob from Crisis Under Control. I ordered chili on salad, a terrible mistake. On my way to the bathroom I bumped into a vagabond guy who had a beautiful tattoo of a woman on his forearm, like a faded Vargas pin-up from the '30s. When I asked him about it, he mumbled so softly that I had to watch his lips to understand him.

"I was in Munich in World War 2," he said. "There was a tattooist there and it was very cheap."

"At the end of the war?" I asked.

"Oh yes," he said, then rambled in his whispered way about the war, saying "fraulein" a lot. I walked away and he didn't stop talking.

In the restroom, I took the messiest shit of 1993.

Back at the House of Hardcore, I fell asleep for a few hours before being awakened by an unrelenting, obnoxious knocking at the door. Sure enough, a cop.

"A city ordinance prohibits these vehicles from being parked on the lawn," he said, standing at the doorway. He meant Ethan's van and Anthony's truck. It was 7 a.m.

"Yes sir," Rob said. "We'll take care of it right now."

The cop scanned the room, observing us crashed on the floor.

"How many people live here?" he asked me.

"How the hell should I know?" I said, more asleep than awake.

"A city ordinance prohibits unlawful over-occupancy of any dwelling within city limits," he said.

A city ordinance should prohibit asshole cops at 7 a.m.

Rob straightened it out, but we were mad at being awakened so early. "If I wasn't so tired, I'd kick that cop in the balls," Ethan said, falling back asleep in seconds.

My throat was sore and I drank some of Chuck's discount cough syrup. It tasted like the polluted run-off of a sugar factory. Chuck, whose throat had been sore for weeks, read the directions wrong and drank four times the adult dosage.

"If my lips turn blue, slap me," he said. His lips weren't blue but I slapped him anyway.

Before leaving the Crisis Under Control crew, Scott told me my flat-top was looking "too Eraserhead." Having brought our clippers on tour, I chopped some off in the House of Hardcore bathroom, apologizing to Rob for any bits of hair I might have left around the sink.

I have this weird theory about my hair: as it grows longer, all of the metaphysical entanglements flying around in the world — alienation, fear, resentment, the usual villains — latch on to the hair strands like dandelion spores to a window screen. This emotional garbage gets embedded in my scalp, mere millimeters from my brain.

When I shave the hair off, I'm revitalized, unreined. A soft, even layer of velour-like fuzz covers the back and sides of my skull, while all of those invisible seeds of negativity lay buzzing in hairy little clumps on the floor, safely away from my head. With my hair newly and cleanly cut, I always feel better and can deal with the world a little easier. That's my theory, anyway.

Departing the House of Hardcore for Athens, Ga., we stopped at a Waffle House despite my pleas otherwise; my alternative, a nearby Cambodian restaurant, made my bandmates visibly retch. This time I ordered the "Scattered, Scrambled & Smothered Hashbrowns" — they left out "Flogged, Raped and Dismembered" — with tomatoes, cheese, onions, ham, various scraps off the kitchen floor, diced stray cat from the back alley and (I think) the chef's left index finger.

Arriving in Athens, we headed for the home of Ethan's friends, Amy and Mel, an intriguing pair of Athens art students, who were putting us up. Anthony, who brought his skateboard on tour, decided to skate down the gigantic hill in front of their house and ate shit three-quarters of the way down, thoroughly shredding the skin on the back of his forearm. It produced a nasty road rash that would get infected and bother him for the rest of the tour.

The Athens air must have been heavy with pollen or ragweed or some airborne spore from hell because my allergies were going haywire. I was scamming napkins from every restaurant in town to sop up the steady stream of snot from my nose. We waited at a bar to meet Wyatt, our former tour companion, who was living somewhere in Athens. Chuck and I found some discarded brooms and an empty pack of cigarettes and started playing street hockey with them. The upper-crust students walking into the bar scowled as we shot the cigarette pack between their legs. Wyatt never came, so we headed for a nearby club to see Sebadoh.

During the show, Anthony, whose allergies were as bad as mine, scored a roll of toilet paper for us, a life saver. The opening band, cult semi-legends Love Child, took the stage, playing average Hendrix-meets-Sonic Youth retro-psychedelic/postmodern chaos pop, straddling the line between sexy and wank. Polvo, a band who'd played in Florida a few weeks before, then assaulted us with their strangely structured, obsessively amelodic, disjointed math rock. Every song sounded like each member was playing the wrong notes at the wrong time, yet in perfectly orchestrated precision. It was the sonic equivalent of a long, complex algebra problem, and it left me a little dizzy.

Finally it was Sebadoh's turn. The club was jammed, and before even strumming his first chord, frontman Lou Barlow threw a pitcher of beer from the stage, drenching a portion of the audience. Someone, it seems, would not stop calling him "an ugly cunt."

"Don't buy my records, motherfucker," Barlow said, sneering.

"Don't by mine, either," said Jason the bassist, mocking Barlow.

As expected, Sebadoh's music was alternately obnoxious and gentle, irritating and sweet. Chuck and I called for songs by Barlow's old band Dinosaur Jr., while Athens locals, being the hip scenesters they are, frowned at us. To increase everyone's irritation, we started yelling fictitious song titles.

"*Greasy Fork!*" Chuck yelled.

"'Greasy fork?'" Barlow repeated into the mike, squinting his eyes at the audience in the darkness. "Who sings 'Greasy Fork?'" He looked back to his band members. "You know 'Greasy Fork?'"

"*Chapstick!*"

"'Chapstick?'" Barlow said. "These are our songs?"

"*Butt Juice!*"

"Shut up!"

"*Big Onion!*"

"SHUT THE FUCK UP!"

At one point, Barlow, twisting his finger up his nostril, announced: "I'm not going to play another song until I get this booger out of my nose." I threw a wadded tissue on stage, still wet with my own snot. As Barlow picked it up and wiped his nose, I could see my snot bubbling out the side.

"Thanks," he said. I guess his allergies were bad too.

We were impressed how, for a band of their cultish popularity, they played through small, unprofessional equipment and weren't too uptight about their performance. They rarely began a song together on time; at one point the drummer wouldn't start at all because he hadn't finished his cigarette. And when a song seemed to be going well, one of them would intentionally mess it up, just for grins. It was quite inspiring actually, a reminder for us not to take ourselves so rock'n'roll seriously.

Returning to Amy's house at 2 a.m., everyone went to sleep but me. I sat alone outside with Amy's cool black dog, Petri, eating Italian cookies and drinking spring water, admiring the incredible clarity of the Georgia night, listening to unseen trains chugging along in the distance. Then I envisioned aliens landing on the front yard and pulling me into their spaceship. I got spooked and went inside. Scott's dementia is spreading.

The next morning everybody thought I'd jack off when I took a shower, not even making it past my second tour stop, but I didn't. In downtown Athens, Chuck and I went to a local art museum, checking out stark woodcuts by Felix Vallatton depicting old Parisian street life. Later we returned to Amy's and took pictures of Fluffy by clotheslines.

The club where we were playing was called Hoyt Street North, and it was decorated somewhat like an old saloon. Exploring the nearby train tracks elevated on a hill, we met some 11-year-old redneck kids who told us their hobby was "fucking girls." I threw rocks with them at a passing train, aiming for the identification numbers on the sides of boxcars. Anthony and Scott chastised me because the rocks were ricocheting off the train and hitting them. The kids thought this was funny and continued doing it.

At the club, we watched as other bands unloaded their equipment. One was called — I can barely stand to repeat it — Fuzzy Sprouts. I asked the manager if we could play first so we didn't have to stick around for the neo-hippie agony that would surely be the Fuzzy Sprouts. He said fine.

In the bar, I played Galaga, my favorite video game in fifth grade, for almost 45 minutes on one quarter. I spun a few rounds of the club's Rolling Stones pinball machine before it caught me tilting, and read an issue of *Circus* magazine that was sitting on the soundboard. Everybody else got drunk.

We took the stage at 10 p.m. Wyatt arrived with a friend during our first song. They were rocking out with Bill, Ethan and Anthony; the remainder of Hoyt Street North's patrons were sitting at the bar or playing cards on the upper level. Between songs they'd sarcastically yell: "Hooray."

"Say, how's that card game going?" I asked.

No response.

"What're you playing? Go-Fish?"

"Poker," somebody said from the rafters.

"What's the game?"

"Queen and the Card After."

"How much you got down?"

No response.

"C'mon!" I said.

"Ten bucks."

"Funny, that's how much it costs to buy all three of our 7-inch records and a T-shirt."

"No thanks."

"A Spoke shirt will get you laid a lot faster than a game of poker."

"No thanks."

During our short set, I broke a string, which, on-stage and without a back-up guitar, is always traumatic, even with only six people in the audience. Pulling off the broken string, struggling with any remaining pieces in the bridge of the guitar, finding the right string in a new set amongst your guitar stuff, putting it on fast, tuning it (which, without the Li'l Geek, would've taken us the rest of the night), and breaking it in by strumming it hard and fast for a half-minute — it's a minor nightmare. What made this situation horrific, however, was the incredibly bad jokes Chuck and Scott felt compelled to tell.

"What's the worst thing about being a child molester?" Scott asked the near-empty room while I frantically tightened my new Dean Markley A string, hoping I could get it on before he got to the punchline. "Cleaning the blood out of the clown suit!"

You could almost hear the bartender breathing. I wanted to crawl under the stage.

We were given $30. We thanked the manager for his generosity and left for Wyatt's house, where we watched some movies by his film-student friends. I fell asleep so fast, I didn't remove the sweat-drenched shirt from the show. It dried stiff.

We left Athens the next morning. During the drive, I read the newest issue of *Cometbus**, which I picked up at an Athens comic book shop, before arriving at Rockafella's, a club in Columbia, S.C. We were welcomed by the security guard, a huge Motorhead-looking guy named Warchild, and the overweight, obnoxious, shit-talking soundman whom we would come to call The Human Pig. He had a mohawk pulled back into a ponytail (a "bolo"), and he wouldn't stop bitching about what a crappy place Columbia is.

Scott Dempsey, our man in Columbia, showed up. He had booked our last concert there, and his current band, Stretch Armstrong, was opening the show, integrating reggae, ska, even Mexican flavors into a tough-guy, Agnostic Front-ish hardcore style.

Before our set, this blond, spiky-haired kid, maybe 15, walked up to me. "Are you Jon?"

"Yup," I replied.

"You don't know me," he said. "I taped your record from a friend who bought it last time you guys were here. I just wanted to let you know that you're... well, Spoke's become one of my favorite bands. I'm glad you guys made it back."

"You're kidding," I said.

"No, really. I listen to you guys pretty much every day. Hey, did you bring any new records?"

I was dumbstruck. Who'd ever think we would become anybody's favorite band? At his age, I used to do the same thing with the nobody bands I loved. I tried to act composed, thanking him heartily and giving him our new 7-inch, but I really didn't know what to say. It's difficult expressing such appreciation.

During our set, the kids in the audience, few beyond high-school age, were going full-throttle, bouncing off the walls, absolutely shredding the place. We played almost flawlessly, except Scott broke a bass string — just as he had done in Columbia the year before — and I had to fill the time with dumb anecdotes. When the spotlight's on, my mind always empties, and all I can think of are dull stories from my childhood (which is still better than child-molester jokes).

"When I was five and in kindergarten," I said into the mike, "I was running up these brick steps during recess and I fell on my chin, right on the edge of a step. It didn't really hurt and I didn't think much of it, just kept on playing. Then all the other kids started screaming and running away from me, and I thought it was a game and I ran after them, and then they *really* panicked. I was like,

---

* The paragon of all punk zines. Every issue of *Cometbus* is a literary event. Truthfully, it deserves your attention far more than this book does.

'What the hell?' It dawned on me that something was wrong, and I put my hand on my chin, and when I looked at my hand it was covered with blood, from the fingertips to the palm. I thought: 'Oh my god, did I smash my chin open?' I looked down to try to see my chin, and the top of my shirt, from my collar down, was bloody. I got scared and started screaming and running with the rest of the kids, trying to run away from *myself*. At the hospital, while they stitched me up, I remember thinking how demented it was that they were able to sew my skin. I still have the scar. What a fucked-up day."

The kids in the audience didn't quite know what to make of that.

"Anyway," I continued, "this next song's called 'Hollowspeak' and it's got nothing to do with any of that."

As a matter of courtesy, we always tried to thank the person behind the soundboard during our set, as such club personnel are rarely acknowledged from the stage. Out of gratitude, they'd often give us the best possible sound in return. The Human Pig was so moved by our praise that, in a fit of mixing-board glee, he put an echo with a 12-second delay on my vocals. Whatever I said or sang would return at full volume 12 seconds later, completely ruining our songs. Dumbass.

The Rockafella's management dealt solely with Dempsey, and he returned from the back office handing me a big wad of cash. Keeping only $10 for his troubles, he gave the entire night's earnings to us and refused to take any for himself, despite our protests.

"You guys are on tour," he said. "You need it."

"Dempsey," I said, "you're a prince among men."

We made pasta and played motorcycle video games at Dempsey's apartment as friends and scenesters stopped by. We were then driven to some giant sand dunes on the outskirts of town, where local kids ride the 50-foot cliffs (sloping at 70-degree angles) on hydroboards. It looked fast and painful, but Dempsey assured me that even if I crashed it was pretty soft.

I watched Anthony try it, then Scott. Both slid down the cliff and landed smoothly.

"Jon!" Scott yelled from the bottom. "You've got to try this! It's incredible!"

I sat on the hydroboard, peering over the edge of the cliff into the sandy abyss below.

Holy Jesus, I thought. This is suicide.

"Fuck that," I said.

"C'mon!" Scott said.

"If you wipe out, you'll just get a mouthful of sand," Dempsey said. "It's not as bad as it looks."

I felt the same gnarl in my stomach as the first time I dropped in on a halfpipe almost a decade before, when my skateboard shot out and I landed in the flat on my tailbone. I almost puked from the pain.

"Someone give me last rights," I muttered.

I pushed off and grabbed the hydroboard under me. My colon leapt into my esophagus as I slid down the cliff at light speed.

I tumbled and took a mouth full of sand.

"See, it's not that bad," Dempsey said. "Just keep your balance. Try it again."

No, it wasn't that bad. It was actually kind of fun. So I spit the sand off my tongue and did it again.

I crashed.

Again.

Crashed.

Again.

Crashed.

By now Scott and Anthony were taking the cliff backwards, turning 180 degrees in mid-slide, practically doing handstands. When we left, I had yet to make a successful run.

"Why can't I do it?" I asked the group. "What am I, a moron?"

Nobody answered.

The next morning, I flossed for the first time on tour. My gums bled like crazy. Seeing the blood go down the drain was like the shower scene in *Psycho*. I have the gums of a horror film.

During lunch, we went to a city park with cascading fountains. Some sort of festival was going on, packing the park with families and strollers. Dave, the dreadlocked guitarist of Stretch Armstrong, thought this would be a good opportunity to show us a trick he and his cohorts called "The Hardcore Reality," in which he:

1. Finds a water source he can sit in.
2. Removes his pants, sits in the water.
3. "Sucks" the water up his butt (i.e., "inverse flatulence").
4. Pulls his pants up, carrying the water in his rectum.
5. Walks around, finds a target.
6. Removes his pants, bends over.
7. Expels the water out of his butt at a high rate of speed. (Dave claimed he could shoot a stream "about 10 feet.")

This Hardcore Reality thing sounded entertaining. I'd heard of similar stunts performed in 19th-century French degenerate theater. We asked Dave what a suitable target would be.

"I don't know," he said. "I'll just shoot at a group of people."

Oh, this was going to be *amazing*.

But as Dave sat naked in one of the fountains (in full public view), the "intake" wasn't going so well. Apparently all conditions must be right for The Hardcore Reality to actually become a reality, or as Dave put it: "Sometimes, if I have to take a shit, I can't do it. And I guess I have to take a shit."

We soon left Dempsey and the rest of his crew from the park and made our way to North Carolina, passing the current hotbed of indie rock, Chapel Hill (our show fell through there), for the more overlooked town of Greensboro. We were staying with Sean Latrelle, a warm, bright guy with whom Crump went to art school. He lived in a cool apartment — some kind of refurbished factory — with his beautiful sister Heidi, who seemed to have no problem with our crass jokes or persistent stench. "Remember, I live with Sean," she said.

With Heidi was her well-coiffed yuppie boyfriend Jimmy. For reasons unknown, Jimmie spent a great deal of time talking about himself to me — his job, his new car, his education, his bright future, his exercise schedule, his theories on cutting welfare to unwed mothers, everything. When I'd walk away, he'd follow me and continue talking. I didn't spend a minute alone in Greensboro. I wanted to kill him.

We arrived at the Infiniti Club early and met the strange, pseudo-military guy who booked our show, a Gomez Adams in army fatigues. The room harbored the usual assortment of punk-club props: cigarette-burned carpet; a disco ball with most mirrors chipped; an unstable, foot-tall wooden stage; a bad P.A. Being a Tuesday, we figured nobody would come so none of it really mattered.

As we set up, a clean-cut guy wearing khaki shorts and a Polo shirt rode his 10-speed bike into the club about an hour before show time. He got off his bike in front of the stage and proceeded to *dance* with it. He pirouetted holding the 10-speed tenderly, like they were a ballet team. Suspicious, we kept our distance.

After a few minutes, he dropped his bike to the floor and sat on the box of Spoke records.

"Move it, asshole!" said Ethan, guarding our stuff. The guy tumbled to the floor and, with his back on the ground, raised both legs in the air, shook them violently and yelled:

"Thank you, God! Thank you!"

Then:

"Fuck me, God! Fuck me!"

Everyone in the club stopped what they were doing.

"That," said the club owner, "is what 50 hits of ecstacy will do to a man."

Then, as quickly as he fell into this state, he pulled out of it. Whatever was going on with him stopped. He rose from the floor, lit a cigarette casually and walked towards the front door, like nothing happened.

He made it about halfway out.

"Oh God!" he yelled, spazzing on the floor again. *"Fuck me!"*

The police arrived, dragged him to his feet and pulled him outside, shoving him into a cop car by way of slamming his head into the roof first.

The show hadn't started and already we were upstaged.

Despite the horrible sound, we were playing well — avoiding mistakes, jumping all over, cracking jokes. The crowd didn't seem to be having nearly as good of a time; they sat in chairs, watching without reaction. Anthony even got on stage to do his "Rapping Clown" bit, where he would don sunglasses and the rainbow-colored afro wig — the one Pat Hughes wore on Halloween for SpoKISS — and, in a gravelly Fred Sanford voice, would deliver this terrible rap:

I saw a tractor coming down the street
So I got out of the way
I ate pizza for dinner tonight
And I still have indigestion
RAPPIN' CLOWN IN DA HOUSE!

We were laughing to tears. The audience shifted uncomfortably in their seats. It was like playing to a county school board.

We could tell we weren't wanted, so we bowed out and let Latrelle take command. Armed with only an acoustic guitar, a capable voice and a handful of folk songs, he blew our set away. The rest of the audience seemed pretty indifferent — people yelled at each other and beer bottles clinked in the background while he sang and strummed alone — but I thought his performance was stellar, one of the best of the tour.

If Latrelle appealed to the highest mentality at the Infiniti Club, the next band, a duo called Vile, undoubtedly catered to the lowest.

The "musician" half of Vile was a skinhead-looking guy who pounded away at a ramshackle bass guitar (the pick-ups were hanging by wires from the frame) through a ready-for-the-junkpile amp. For the whole set, he had to hold his right foot up against the amp in a twisted, awkward position to keep the chord in. Occasionally he'd lose his balance and fall.

Vile's other member was a guy who looked like Doug Henning with thick, ugly eyeglasses and an uglier Hawaiian shirt. While the skinhead guy played sloppy, over-modulated bass lines, the Doug Henning guy addressed the crowd individually:

"Fuck you, Joe! You're an asshole!... Fuck you, Fred! I'll kick your fucking ass!... Fuck you, Tim! Everybody knows you're queer! Why don't you just come out and admit it!..."

Then he'd pull out a harmonica and blow one note as hard as he could into the microphone, piercing the already suffering eardrums of the Infiniti Club's patrons.

As if on command, the audience retaliated. They hurled cups, bottles, paper, ashtrays, garbage, anything they could find towards the stage. Though the two members of Vile ducked and swerved the objects deftly, they would not stop playing.

Vile made it through about five songs until the Doug Henning guy announced: *"This next song's dedicated to Ronnie and that fat whore he sleeps with! It's called 'Big-Tittied Mama'!"*

Ronnie, evidently present, yelled "fuck you" and picked up a barstool, throwing it at the stage and nailing the already ailing bass amp.

Goodnight Vile.

We packed our stuff and drove back to Latrelle's, a little stunned by the evening's events. At his apartment, as I inched towards slumber on the floor, I fell asleep confident that I would see no band in my lifetime more entertaining than the fiasco that was Vile.

The next day there was some discussion about venturing out to John Coltrane's birthplace nearby, but we never did. Ethan did his laundry and inadvertently threw a new red shirt in the wash, turning his entire load pink. He was pissed.

After hitting a neighborhood pizza shop and book stores, we left Greensboro for a show with Avail in Richmond, Va. We were originally booked for a venue in Richmond, but Tim, Avail's singer, told us it was owned by "a card-carrying member of the Ku Klux Klan," and that Richmond's punk community had boycotted it.

"Just our luck," I said.

"Hey, no problem," Tim said. "Play at our place with us."

For the drive, it was a dreary, sunless day, the perfect excuse for me to sleep through the entire trip. When I awoke hours later, we were parked on an unevenly paved, tree-lined street. I correctly assumed we made it to Virginia. Upon arriving at Avail's house — a semi-trashed two-story Victorian on a street with one of the largest populations of mentally ill people per capita in the country, I later learned — we were greeted by the whole troop of Avail kids, all very friendly.

Carrying my amp to the second-floor, however, I was confronted with an unexpectedly menacing, sinister presence. At the top of the long staircase was the silhouette of two dogs peering down at me. Their breed was unmistakable.

Pit bulls.

Danger! Danger! Danger!

I have no love for any animal with a locking jaw, an animal that's psychotic from generations of in-breeding yet isn't locked in a zoo. Having observed more than a few pit bulls snap into "Hitler mode," I make a point to keep a healthy distance from them, like 30 or 40 miles.

As I heaved my amp up the last stair, figuring I could drop it on them if they attacked, the two hellhounds sniffed me distrustfully as I snuck by.

"N-n-nice doggie," I quavered.

One pit bull yawned, the other shuffled away. Whew.

I piled my equipment in a corner and explored the house. It was in rough shape, as Avail were moving out, cleaning and making last-minute repairs — tearing down lofts, painting over grafitti — in hopes of reclaiming some of their security deposit.

"Fuck the deposit!" I said. "Live free!" They were unconvinced.

Meeting Beau, Avail's "cheerleader," was memorable. I was in the living room with Chuck, who was busy positioning his drums, when Beau jumped at us. Standing in nothing but dingy underwear briefs, tattooed from head to toe, displaying a profusion of piercings, Beau bore a long, unruly, green goatee, a dreadlocked mohawk and a mischievous grin that said: 'I may not hurt you — *but I could.*'

"Greetings!" he said, his hands pointed in the U-shaped Satanic sign in our faces, twiddling his outstretched pinkies and forefingers. "Welcome to Richmond. I'm Beau!"

Tim said Beau and his cheerleading skills are as essential to the band as Eric the drummer or Joe the guitarist. He works the crowd, sings back-up, beats on drums and does flips on the stage, sometimes with pom-poms.

"Anthony does Rapping Clown," I said to Tim. "That's sort of like a cheerleader, only he makes everybody *leave.*"

By 8 o'clock, we took over Avail's empty living room, about 20 feet wide and 15 feet long. The big fear was that the hardwood floor, buckling after years of abuse and disrepair, would collapse under the weight of our equipment, the audience and us, and we'd find ourselves with broken legs in the kitchen of the apartment 20 feet below. We jumped on the floor to gauge its stability; it displayed considerable flex. This would be interesting.

About 50 people packed in the room. Wisely, they sat down. As we jumped and flailed during our set, I came damn close to falling on a few kids seated in front and smacking others with the head of my guitar as I spun around. Between songs, these much tattooed and pierced folks kindly asked me to "please be careful."

When Avail played, the room exploded. Melodic, thundering and uplifting, Avail's music was setting the standard nationwide for post-hardcore, pop-infused rock. The temperature had risen so high that condensation was forming on the walls. Towards the end of the set, Beau and Tim started jumping on the floor like mad, causing an exodus from the room. It seemed the pair were hellbent on breaking the floor — and judging by the way it was caving in, it looked like they would. By luck, it held.

Needing a break from the crowd and chaos, I slinked over to a couch to relax and catch up on some tour writing. I was interrupted by a scratchy female voice.

"You guys weren't bad."

She had choppy, fire-engine red hair, two hoops symmetrically penetrating her bottom lip amid other facial piercings, a tight little-league baseball shirt over plaid pajama pants, and a bottle of Bacardi in her hand. Her pupils swooped from one side of her sockets to the other, and her eyelids stood at half-mast.

"Thanks," I said. "We had fun. This is a great place."

"No it's not."

"Oh. Okay."

"What're you writing there?" she asked.

"A little document of the tour, I guess," I said.

"What for?"

"A zine, maybe. Or just to remember it. Or maybe a book sort-of-thing later on."

"A book? About your band?"

"Maybe."

"That's the stupidest thing I've ever heard," she slurred.

"Excuse me?"

She laughed.

"More fucking suburban white boys trying to write how fucking important punk rock is," she said, shaking her head. "Who do you think wants to read some crap about your band anyway?"

"I don't know."

"Fuck, man, what makes you special? Why should anybody give a shit about dumb boys making dumb music for other dumb boys?"

"You just said we weren't bad."

"Fuck you."

Jesus, what did I do to deserve this? "Listen," I said, getting up, "I'm leaving. Have a nice night."

"Right," she said, then added as I walked away:

"Guys like you are ruining punk rock."

Fuming, I stomped into another room and found Scott. "Man, this crazy drunk bitch just—"

"Did you call Kim Coletta?" he asked.

"Uh, no."

"Call Kim Coletta."

"Oh. Right."

I got through to Kim, who played bass in Jawbox and was giving us a place to crash for our Washington, D.C. show. I tried to get directions, but with a bad phone line and party noise drowning out every other syllable, progress was slow.

"Kim, I can't hear a thing you're saying," I yelled. "Can you start again?"

The static broke up up her words: *"Wer... ew... frah... ichman..."*

"Huh?"

"Ah... en... itchin..."

"Kitchen? I'm nowhere near the kitchen."

"RICHMOND! RICHMOND! WHERE ARE YOU COMING FROM IN RICHMOND?" The line was suddenly clear.

"Oh... well, I don't know, really..."

"Dit... fra... so..." The phone went crackly again, and continued that way for a half-hour.

Later, Tim stopped me as I was storing Chuck's drums in a safe corner. He had collected donations and gave me the night's total: $94.

"Dude, that's unbelievable," I said. "You've got to take some."

"Fuck you," Tim said, smiling, pushing the wad of bills to me. "Take it."

"No, man. It's your house."

"Fuck you. Take it."

"Please, more people came to see you than us," I said. "Have half."

"Fuck you. Take it."

"But—"

"Fuck you. Take it."

There was no point in arguing. I gave him a hug and took it.

After the party fizzled, we went to sleep on musty mattresses bound for the garbage dump amid dust bunnies that had overtaken the bare, unswept floor. The mattresses were really gross — Ethan expressed concern we all might get crabs — but I was glad to be sleeping on a cushion at all, even if it felt (and smelled) like it was filled with dung. The only thing masking its stench was my own.

I had a great dream that night, surely brought on by my total lack of sexual contact. I was a king (or something), and I was in this huge, bizarre, medieval bed between a pair of gorgeous Asian girls who were treating me, well, royally. But when I awoke that morning, there was indeed a pair with me in bed — and it wasn't Asian girls.

Danger! Danger! Danger!

The pit bulls were lying with me, sniffing my face, no doubt getting a taste before making a meal of me. Figuring this was how lions toy with their prey before ripping them to meaty shreds, I played dead. Then Tim walked in.

"Hey, a ménage-à-trois," he said.

"Tim, your goddamn dogs are trying to eat me."

"No, man. They like you. Go ahead, pet them. They're showing their affection."

Afraid that if I spurned them they'd bite me out of spite, I patted their boxy skulls and, sure enough, they settled down. Putting their heads on the cushion between their front paws and basking in my attention, they actually looked cute, not at all the jaw-locking beasts of Armageddon I had come to expect. I began to re-think my stance on pit bulls.

Having secured directions, we thanked the entire Avail crew as we packed for the short drive to D.C. Unfortunately, Tim, who found my chaste ways on tour highly comical, did the disservice of giving us three porno mags that he found in the heaps of Avail house trash.

"I'm helping your cause, making you strengthen your willpower," he said wryly. "Really."

During the trip to D.C., flipping through these magazines *punished* me. My groin was literally aching to be rid of its vicious lust. It was awful.

We entered Silver Springs, Md., where Jawbox lived. I was looking forward to seeing them; having promoted a number of Jawbox shows in Gainesville, we had grown to be friends. They welcomed us with hugs and pasta, as Kim was making a batch of tomato-mushroom sauce as we arrived. Guitarists Bill and J. showed us their basement practice space, resembling as much of a professional studio as Tommy's, and we immediately inquired about the status of their major-label signing to Atlantic Records, of which we (as well as they) were a little skeptical.

An hour later, Zach, their drummer, came home. I got along well with everyone in Jawbox, but I had the strongest connection with Zach. His wit, integrity and congeniality were punctuated by great idiosyncrasies: his rapid-fire speech, his crooked Dead End Kid smile, his dominant eye cocked wider than the other, and his ability to seamlessly slip lines from *Raging Bull* into common conversation. ("Okay, we'll go to the Thai restaurant for lunch and *I'll get youse both in the fuckin' ring and I'll give youse both a fuckin' beating and youse both can fuck each other.*")

After eating, Zach took us to the bookshop where he worked. Apparently he and his coworkers shared a strong resentment towards their stingy, mean (and usually absent) boss, so they stole books freely.

"Go ahead, take some," Zach said. "Everybody here turns a blind eye to it and does it themselves. If the owner wasn't such a hateful bastard, we wouldn't do it. But he is, so we do. Free books — all yours."

"No, man," I said. "We can't."

"Please. We *want* you to have them."

"This boss of yours must be a real dick."

"He is. Take some books."

"I don't want you to get in trouble, Zach."

"If you guys don't walk out of this store with books, I'm kicking all your asses," he said. "It's Christmas morning. Have as many as you want."

This was a dangerous proposition. Scott and I are book junkies, and offering us a whole bookstore was like giving a dedicated pothead a paid vacation to Humboldt County. After an hour of perusing the shelves, we each left with five to 10 titles, filling about four shopping bags. Scott nabbed the best score, a first-edition *Death in Midsummer and Other Stories* by Yukio Mishima in mint condition (which he would accidentally spill grape juice all over a few days later). Even by the store employees' loose standards, it was a memorably large heist.

The next day we hit the Smithsonian, spending a lot of time at the Vietnam Memorial, always an essential D.C. stop. The tens of thousands of names on the wall silenced us all, granting us an immediate sense of perspective. It might sound self-absorbed, but whenever I visit the Vietnam Memorial, I'm always faced with the same conclusion: my name could have been etched on that black wall, as could any of my friends' names. But we were lucky enough to be born later, to not have to face fighting a pointless, costly war.

There was an exhibit at the Museum of American History of mementos that had been left at the Vietnam Memorial since its construction. It was a poignant assortment: cigarettes; cans of beer; combat boots; bullets; a patch with Snoopy saying, "Fuck it, just fuck it"; a Congressional Medal of Honor returned in protest of Ronald Reagan's Central American policies; a bottle of Jack Daniels; photos of soldiers in rice fields with Vietnamese peasants; homemade sculptures; baby shoes; flowers; and a huge array of heart-wrenching cards, notes and letters.

Eventually we made our way to the White House. I was hellbent on getting one of our records to Bill Clinton. I concluded long ago that the President of the United States *must* own a Spoke record.

Everybody has their gripes with Clinton, as do I. But having spent the preceding decade in ardent opposition to Reagan, Bush and the rest of their hypocritical, elitist, self-serving ilk, Clinton's election was the first time I felt any real hope for America's political future. Plus, from a strictly personal standpoint, I simply had to support the presidency of an Elvis fan whose favorite food is enchiladas and who can play Thelonious Monk on the saxophone. Sure beats the hell out of "Just Say No."*

I walked to the White House gate and tried to hand our *Seratonin* 7-inch record to a guard. He told me in no uncertain terms to take my arm out of the gate and bring it to the mailroom in the Executive Administration Building down the street.

"That's where gifts are received," the guard said. "Take 'em over there. We don't want 'em."

At the Executive Administration Building, the public mailroom for the president was in the basement. There, across a counter, I stood face to face with a real Washington bureaucrat, a guy about my age but better dressed.

"So, you ever met the president?" I said, handing him our record.

"Yes," he said. "He came in this office and shook my hand."

"And he gave a heartfelt greeting, like: 'Good work, son.'"

"Yes, I believe so."

"He sounds like a nice guy, then."

---

* Of course, this was before Clinton fumbled the issue of gays in the military, dropped the fight for nationwide health care, bombed the living hell out of Iraq so routinely that the press stopped covering it, buckled under a "Republican revolution" that lasted all of two years, and got sucked off by a tacky, catty intern. Oh yeah: and got impeached.

"Yes."

"What about Hillary?"

"I've not met the First Lady."

"Do you think she's hot?"

"Excuse me?"

"Do you think Hillary Clinton is hot?"

He looked at me uncomfortably.

"Why do you ask?"

"Just curious," I said. "I think she's a dish."

"Well, I suppose Mrs. Clinton is an attractive woman, yes."

"So, does an armored car come here and pick up the mail?"

"No, I walk it over myself."

"To the White House? Like in a box?"

"Yes. Or we put it in a bag."

"Don't they worry about terrorists stealing the president's mail?"

He looked away, giving the issue a second's thought, and said: "I guess not."

"Say," I said, "if there was a nickel bag in the record sleeve, would it get through?"

"A nickel bag?"

"Yeah."

He looked at the record, thin and flat. "A bag of nickels is in this record?"

Oh, *shit*.

"No, man," I said. "Pot. *A bag of marijuana*. You know, Clinton and all..."

He looked at me very seriously. This was the most humorless youngster in America.

"There's pot in here?" he asked gravely.

"Never mind," I said, walking off. "If you could be sure it gets to him, I'd appreciate it."

I don't know if it ever got through. We never received a letter from the White House thanking us for the gift. I figure it was probably intercepted to be checked for lyrical content. I thrilled at the thought of stone-faced G-men listening to our record, carefully examining the words for subliminal messages that might alter presidential policy and endanger national security. *Hey Bill! 666! Fellatio! Cigars! Whoo!*

Returning to Silver Springs, we ate at an Eisenhower-era chrome diner near Jawbox's house. All of the waitresses had huge jellyroll flesh packed into light green uniforms and had their hair neatly bundled in hairnets; they called you "shugah" and chewed gum with their mouths open. On the jukebox, we played Patsy Cline and Merle Haggard, and slopped down chicken and dumplings, meatloaf and chicken fried steak. I wanted to move in.

The next afternoon we shoved off to Georgetown for our show. Though Jawbox couldn't attend — they were playing in Baltimore that afternoon — we invited other acquaintances living in the D.C. area, including Fugazi, who had stayed at SpokeHouse the year before.

I think all contemporary D.C. bands — all postcore bands world-wide, actually — owe major gratitude to Fugazi. I could fill many pages on Fugazi's subcultural significance, why they're such an important group to so many people, and why they are, in my estimation, the best rock band to emerge in a decade. But plenty has been said about them already — their unwavering ethics, pioneering sound, unconventionally low pricing structures, political conviction and against-the-grain popularity are well-documented, even in the mainstream rock press — and much more will be written in the years to come. For me, Fugazi redefined and revitalized everything in punk rock — hell, in art itself — and it wouldn't surprise me if, 50 years from now, people speak of them with the same reverence as they do the Velvet Underground, Miles Davis, Robert Johnson and other musical visionaries.

We arrived at the Mountain Lodge, the small coffee shop that was hosting the show. The guy running the place — tall, mid-30s, sort of professorial-looking — was still moving tables and chairs to one side as we walked in. He didn't seem happy to see us.

"I don't know where you plan to put this stuff," he said, pointing to our amps, "but they're not coming in here until you play."

So we left our equipment on the curb in front of the Mountain Lodge, partially blocking a narrow sidewalk busy with weekend rollerbladers, joggers and upscale Georgetown shoppers. I sat on one of my Peaveys and changed my guitar strings while surveying the sunny urban scene. Traffic sped in front of us, smelly overstuffed trash cans sat at my side, and a steady stream of yuppies walked by, looking at us and our out-of-place, in-the-way equipment.

When it was time to move in, the manager guy informed me the cafe had no running water and only one AC plug.

"What kind of cafe has no water and limited electricity?" I asked. "How do you make the coffee?"

"This is a poetry cafe," he said.

"Oh."

Given the way we screamed and sweated onstage, having nothing to drink between songs was unfortunate. Far worse was the fact we had to route three amps, two effects pedals and a P.A. through a six-pronged power strip into one electrical outlet. This is just the sort of thing my amps hate. Immediately they squealed, skronked and wailed. And the P.A. was so muffled and crackly that everything I was saying, even without the interference of guitars and drums, was incoherent.

So we tried playing a set. After the first song, the entire audience of 40 folks (all friends of the following band, the straight-edge unit Ashes), went outside. Even I couldn't bear to hear us. Luckily none of the D.C. folks we invited showed up.

We stopped at our sixth song and let Ashes have their fun. We sucked, and that was that.

Hawk, the kid who promoted the concert, was supportive and apologetic, not realizing the venue (or the guy running it) would be such a problem.

"I can't budge a cent from him," Hawk said. "I could maybe give you $25."

"Man," I said, "given the way we sounded, that would be charity." We thanked him, loaded up and left immediately for Philadelphia.

In our not-so-wise manner of booking, we scheduled a show in Philadelphia that evening, then a second show in town the next night. Scott's rationale: "Philly's a rock'n'roll town." (That's a Spinal Tap quote.)

Arriving in Philadelphia, we spent nearly an hour driving around a dilapidated Irish neighborhood guarded by pasty-faced kids holding hockey sticks, looking mean and staring us down. We asked some people on a corner about the location of the (brilliantly named) club, the Temple of the Raging Chicken. They told us it wasn't "anywhere around." Naturally, we found it a block away.

We pulled into the driveway of a large warehouse with broken windows. It seemed abandoned except for a lone figure chasing a dog in the parking lot. On closer inspection, he was playing fetch with a mangy German shepherd and a two-by-four. He'd throw the huge wood plank and the dog would either catch it or get knocked on the head.

"That's one tough dog," Ethan said.

The guy ran towards the van. He looked like Charles Manson.

"Hey, you here for the show?" he said. He seemed to have no teeth.

"Yeah," Anthony said from the driver's seat, his window rolled down. "Say, what're you doing with your dog there?"

"We're playing catch," he said, then laughed a crazy laugh that made me nervous. He pointed at the dog: "That's Scrap. I'm Charlie."

Jesus, maybe this *was* Charles Manson.

I got out of the van, walked to the front door (ignoring Charlie), and banged on it with my fist.

"You shouldn't do that," Charlie said. "The people around here don't like noise much."

"Fine place for a punk club then," I said. Charlie laughed his psycho little laugh and walked back to Scrap in the parking lot.

Inside, the guy managing the place — I think his name was Jim — also did sound, security and promotion. The space was impressive, a big open warehouse with four-story ceilings. It was like an airplane hangar with a couple of kegs in one corner and a little stage in the middle.

"Temple of the Raging Chicken is a great name," I said to Jim. "How did you come up with it?"

"I was stoned," he said.

The first band arrived and loaded in. They were called the Guttersnipes or Gutterballs or Gutter-somethings, from New Jersey. They were trying very hard to pull off a '77 punk pose: bondage pants, safety pins in the lips, Sid Vicious snarl, chopped hair, homemade Dead Boys shirts with burn holes. The bassist was a cute, small brunette with an endearing smile. Her name was Darla, and she said she grew up in a town near my high school. As we chatted, my mind was concocting a thousand ways to weasel her into the van to share a private moment together, but she had to leave to play her set. Damn.

When the Gutterwhatevers took the stage, I took note of the Temple's customers: bikers. No punks, hardcore kids, indie rockers, metalheads, or hippies — just bikers. And they were getting *very* drunk.

The green-haired, neck-chained lead singer, "Damien" (a band has to work hard to be this contrived), started cutting his chest with a torn aluminum can and beating the microphone against his face, G.G. Allin-style. Blood covered the microphone and lightly splattered the stage. He broke a bottle on the ground but he wouldn't roll around in the broken glass, so I booed him.

After half an hour, Darla's bass strap broke, sending the bass crashing to the ground. She shrugged and they all walked off the stage — end of set.

After cleaning Damien's blood off the microphone, I stuck a condom over it and sang into the condom for our entire set. I wasn't taking any chances.

We started with one of our heavier songs to gauge the crowd. Most of them stood at a distance looking mean. Then about halfway through the song, Jim walked onto the small stage from the mixing board, found the volume knob on my amp, and turned it down a few notches.

I couldn't believe it. After the song, I leaned over the mixing board to Jim.

"What the fuck did you do that for?"

"The neighbors don't like noise," he said.

"So what? Fuck the neighbors! Don't touch my amp!"

"Dude, they're Irish mob and they don't like noise."

"Fuck the Irish mob!"

I turned the volume knob back up and, midway through the next song, Jim turned it down again. Seeing that I didn't want Jim kneecapped or anything, I left the volume low. Thanks to the Irish mob, our set blew.

Later, as I was putting stuff in the van, I felt a tap on my shoulder. It was Darla.* Her eyes were glazed over. Her body was limply shifting.

"You guys were real... um... *fun*," she said, half-smiling, looking as if she'd fall into a coma on the spot. Then she ambled away.

Some speedmetal band was finishing the show, and by now the vibe at the Temple of the Raging Chicken was slipping into havoc: bottles breaking, a guy puking in the corner, bikers fighting, and a woman everyone called "Mom" (with whom we were supposedly staying) running around shooting hairspray in everyone's hair, screaming: "*I'm killing the ozone! I'm killing the ozone!*"

As I walked into the center of the warehouse's cavernous expanse to pick up my amps, the Gutterwhatevers' drummer said from behind me: "Uh-oh, you're the next victim."

Green-haired Damien pulled me into his arms and started biting my neck.

"You're going to turn into one of them," the drummer said.

"All right, thank you Mr. Vampire," I said, playing along, pushing him away. "That'll do."

Damien kept biting. Hard.

"Get off me, you fuck!" I yelled.

"Don't worry," the drummer said. "He does it to everybody."

He let loose and ran off to bite someone else. I went outside and looked at my neck in the side-door mirror of the van. The bastard

---

* For anyone keeping score, Darla's tap — that millisecond when her finger touched my shoulder — was the most action I'd get on tour.

broke my skin. I could have rabies from this asshole.

I walked into the bathroom to wash my wound. It was one of the sickest bathrooms of any club we played in, with a long urinal trough in the center that someone evidently took a shit in. The sink was another trough, encrusted with mildew. Questionable puddles and spots marked the floor and walls.

At the corner of the bathroom was Darla, surrounded by four people sitting cross-legged and hunched over. I was about to go over and say hello, but she was slumped against the wall in a sideways position, looking asleep. Her circle of cohorts discreetly passed things between them. I deduced they were shooting up. I left.

Despite (or because of) the surrounding chaos, even with a bitten neck and doused sexual hopes, I had to admit I was enjoying this place. Everywhere I looked, something insane was happening. What would happen next?

On my way outside, Jim grabbed me and placed 50 bucks in my hand. I was floored. How did he generate that much cash from a meager crowd of bikers? It was already such a crazy night, I would've been happy to play for nothing.

Chuck and Ethan, however, were less enthusiastic. This was undoubtedly a volatile scene, and the potential for things to go wrong seemed to double every 10 minutes. Crump wasn't happy with the situation either. Scott and Anthony were willing to flow with it, but I was the only one who really wanted to stay.

"I don't like this at all," Ethan said, standing outside the van in an impromptu meeting.

"What are our options?" Anthony said. "Where else can we go in Philly?"

"Can we go to New York now?" Crump said.

"No, we've got another show in town tomorrow," I said.

"Here? In Philadelphia? Why?" Ethan asked.

"It just kind of worked out that way," I said. I didn't want to divulge too much about our boneheaded scheduling.

"I think we should just cancel tomorrow's show," Chuck said, "and get to New York tonight."

Everyone seemed to agree. The idea was attractive, if only because skipping town and hitting New York sounded more fun than spending a second night in Philadelphia. But I reminded them that, ethically, it was a bad move. We would be doing the wrong thing — nixing the other show, leaving the Temple of the Raging Chicken people hanging, screwing over lots of folks — and would probably pay for it somehow later.

"I don't want to hang around here tonight," Chuck said in his quietly assertive way. "I'd rather move on."

So I went back into the club and told Jim we were stepping out to get cheesesteak sandwiches, lying to a man who had just given me $50.

"Hurry back," he said, then shouted to his friends: "We're gonna party all night with Spoke!"

I jumped into the van. We tore through the Irish-mob streets and found the freeway that would get us to New York. With much elation and cheering, we made our way out of Philadelphia at midnight, leaving the Temple of the Raging Chicken and its crazy cast of characters behind us forever, fucking over the City of Brotherly Love. What dicks we were.

With our road atlas, I managed to find the route to the town where my grandparents lived — Mount Vernon, N.Y. — just north of the Bronx. On the New Jersey Turnpike, somebody threw a full Coke can at the van from their car, denting the door. We gladly accepted this minor act of aggression as our karmic retribution for ditching all of those friendly maniacs in Philadelphia.

Having made our way through the maddening cross-borough highways of New York City, we stopped at a pay phone near the worst retail store in the world, a place called Ark Drugs, a few blocks from my grandparents' apartment. Though I notified Grandma and Grandpa Resh a few days before, I was a little worried as to how they would receive a call at 4 a.m. They are, after all, "seniors."

"Hello?" my grandmother answered sleepily.

"Grandma!" I said into the phone. "We're at the Ark!"

"Come on over!" she said.

The six of us piled into their little apartment a few hours before sunrise. My grandparents were thrilled. They are truly saints.

We hung out for the next few days trying to nudge onto a bill at some venues, but, unlike the Hardback, no club in the area — not CBGBs, ABC No Rio, Maxwell's, Pyramid — would add us to their schedule, though we offered to play for free. New York City sucks that way.

So without a show, we bummed around Manhattan. We took photos of Fluffy on Fifth Avenue. Chuck hooted at Brooke Shields walking in Chelsea. We closely observed raw entrails of an unknown animal being sold as food in Chinatown. The Times Square arcade where I bought my first fake I.D. when I was 15 was gone. And I got sick after scarfing a Sabrett's hot dog. Good ol' New York.

The guys were having a good time — Grandma made big meals,

Grandpa talked sports — but with the date of our Louisville, Ky., show nearing, we had to cruise.

"Break a leg," Grandma said to me cheerfully, watching us get in the van. "That means good luck in the theater business. I don't really want you to break a leg."

"I know, Grandma."

"I'll light a candle for your tour and say a prayer," she said.

"Rad."

I slept for most of the drive down, but was awakened as if by instinct upon entering Louisville, the place where I was born.

I was expecting this show to be something of a homecoming, since, having lived in Louisville for the first 13 years of my life, my associations with the town are strong. We were meeting Tim Furnish, my close friend since third grade, who played guitar in the postcore powerhouse Crain. Driving around town, familiar sights bombarded me. Because I visited Louisville rarely, the city was still a childhood land locked in my memory. To see it as an adult was a bit overwhelming.

We were playing at some teen club that hosted punk shows. Another band on the bill, Hoover (from D.C.), were already there and in bad spirits: the day before, while unloading equipment, their van somehow rolled down a hill and hit something. Though the damage wasn't severe, they didn't seem to want to talk about it, understandably.

We assembled our gear on the big stage — almost five-feet high, needlessly tall for a band like us — and started playing early, around 5 p.m. About 20 people were in attendance, including Tim. Despite my excitement to play my old hometown, we sounded terrible. I kept dropping my guitar pick; Chuck's drum kit kept inching away from him as he pounded his kick drum; my amps sounded crackly; and half of the P.A. was out. It was a letdown. Yet we received some applause after each song, perhaps limp and obligatory, but nonetheless a gracious gesture by the small Louisville audience. I appreciated it.

Hoover took the stage and seemed to have it very together. There was, however, something subtly irritating about their performance, something I had yet to witness in any band. It was as if these guys were wearing their emocore credibility on their sleeves.

From the start, people in Gainesville's scene tagged Spoke as an emo band: we played "sincere" punk with noisy, aggressive pop leanings, influenced by Hüsker Dü, Embrace, early Dag Nasty, Gray Matter and the undisputed progenitors of the emocore genre,

Rites of Spring. We sang about emotional issues and didn't give a shit if people thought we were sissies; if that made us "emo," fine. Since emocore itself wasn't yet codified — there was no absolute emo sound, style of dress or any real aesthetic manifesto, at least not in Florida — we didn't care.

But in Hoover, I was seeing a package of emo cliches that would later grow into a burgeoning musical and subcultural category, inevitably caricaturing and diluting itself. To Hoover's credit, what I was sensing was less fashion than nuance, but it was my first whiff of the prefabricated Next Wave of Emo, and it stunk.

Wondering if I was just being snotty, I asked Scott what he thought. "This band is the most derivative thing I've ever seen," he said. "It's Fugazi junior." He obviously sensed it too.

Rodan played last, setting up on the dance floor among the patrons. I had met them the year before through Tim, and found their earlier musical projects to be amazing. Though a little sloppy for this show, Rodan would later grow into one of the great experimental postpunk bands of the '90s, delving further into textured guitar territories pioneered by Sonic Youth and Slint.

Afterwards, the club manager told us she admitted everyone for free. "We wouldn't have had a crowd otherwise," she said. "I thought if some people came in for no charge, you might be able to sell some merchandise."

She got on the microphone and urged the remaining audience to "donate a couple of bucks to the bands" since the show was free. Only one guy did, giving us 75 cents. Scott spent it all on a video game.

We left the club for the Rocket House, home of Crain and Rodan members, where we were staying. For dinner, we had a craving for White Castle hamburgers — cheap, tasty and unavailable in Florida. On our way out, Crump and I saw a guy from Hoover.

"Hey, would you like to join us at White Castle?" I asked.

"No," he said.

"Oh... Are you sure?"

"Yeah."

"Can we pick something up for you?" Bill asked.

"We don't have any money."

"Well, we could spot you," I said.

"No," he said, turning his back to me, and added sternly: "We have our own food."

Jeez, what a grump. But I figured if our van had rolled down a hill and got smashed, I'd be in a bad mood too. Plus, if he were vegan (as many members of emo bands tend to be), the very mention of White Castles would be enough to make him hurl.

Coming back from dinner, another one of the Hoover guys met me at the doorway. He was apparently waiting for us. He seemed miffed.

"Can you get your stuff out of the way here?" he said indignantly. "We need to bring in our equipment."

"Uh, sure," I said.

"A simple 'please' would have been nice," Ethan said under his breath.

Yeah, a "please" would have been nice. But, well, their van did roll down a hill and all.

After moving our amps and drums, I walked into the main room of the Rocket House where some folks were lounging. The conversation revolved around Jawbox, and one of the Hoover guys seemed to assert that Jawbox's recent signing to a major label was a bit cagey. There was a contemplative pause among the group.

"Well, I don't know," I said. "Jawbox may simply have an agenda that differs from —"

"Whatever," the Hoover guy said, dismissively waving his hand — interrupting me, nullifying my statement as if my opinion was so lacking in validity that it wasn't worth being heard, as if my presence was utterly insignificant in the company of a band as superior as Hoover, *as if I was some kind of fuck.*

That was it. Hoover could kiss my white ass. We introduced ourselves to them respectfully and congenially (as we would to anyone), even overlooking their initial brusqueness because some jackass forgot to activate the emergency brake in their van; they in turn treated us with arrogance and aloofness. Hoover then became our tour villains; for the remainder of our travels, they were the reference point for everything shitty in this world. ("Sure, the global proliferation of nuclear armaments does suck — *but not as much as Hoover.*")*

The next afternoon, we ate at one of my favorite childhood haunts, Another Place Sandwich Shop, with Crain's singer and drummer John Cook. When I was 10, there was this cadre of redneck kids who'd hang out in the back room of Another Place and play video games, trying to slug the machines with bus tokens, pushing me around to loosen some of my quarters. I peeked in the

---

* I bumped into one of the Hoover guys a few years later at the Empty Bottle in Chicago. He was very cordial and admitted to "having a really bad night" in Louisville, and we laughed it off. To Hoover: maybe we were all pricks; if apologies are in order, sorry.

back room hoping to find them still sitting on pinball machines 12 years later, now swigging beers and fanning themselves with unemployment checks, but it was empty. We finished eating, left Another Place, dropped John off at Rocket House, and made our way to Detroit.

I knew Detroit would be plush because we were staying at the house of Scott's mom and stepdad for a few days in the affluent suburb of Rochester Hills. After dropping off our bags there, we arrived at the club, Blondie's. Bullet holes peppered its front door, which Scott said was "very Detroit."

We learned we were playing with yet another speedmetal band, except the lead singer of this one had the balls to walk up to me and say:

"Your band has to play first because we're headlining."

I laughed.

"Yeah, sure," I said, shaking my head, making him feel a little foolish. "You do that."

"Headlining" is such a stupid issue. The headliner — the band that "tops" a bill — is assumed to be the important act of the evening, though opening acts always have the potential of being better. Egos flare maniacally when it comes to who headlines: a band is supposed to earn instant prestige from being at the top of the concert hierarchy, from which they will (presumably) have the greatest number of people present to see them. And for bigger shows, headliners are almost always paid more.

But if a band is bad, they're bad no matter where they're slotted. And on a level as small as ours, it didn't make a damn bit of difference who played in what order, and for this speedmetal bonehead to think otherwise was delusional.

Taking the stage, our performance was strangely tight — all of this touring seemed to be paying off — and Blondie's sound system really worked for us. There wasn't much of a crowd, but the people who were there seemed to enjoy themselves, laughing at our dumb between-song banter. "You guys are like a punk *Kids in the Hall*," one girl said after our set — the best compliment of the tour.

Blondie's manager, sullen and dark, seemed like a recent Nine Inch Nails convert. He wasn't outright goth or old-school industrial, but an overnight Winger-turned-Ministry fan, his '80s hair-metal roots still showing. He wasn't very nice.

"Here's your cut," he said, handing me two $10 bills.

"Only 20 bucks, huh?" I said.

"Yeah."

"That's not very much, considering how far from home we are."

"Not many people came tonight."

"What's the split?"

"The bands split half the door."

"And the bar?"

"We keep what we get at the bar."

"And it was four bucks a head?"

"Yeah."

"If the bands' share is half the door, then you're paying us for 20 people, but there were more than 20 people in the club," I said.

"Well, that's all you're getting."

I didn't feel like giving him the tirade I gave the Blue Marlin guy in Miami two years ago. It was a great show, and I was tired and in no mood to cheapen the experience by getting into a shouting match.

"Well, if this means you're not giving us any more money, then—"

"Then what?" he said antagonistically, like he was expecting a fight.

"Then you can go get fucked," I said and walked out.

That felt great.

The next two days we languished in the basement of Scott's mom's house, watching Bruce Lee movies and playing pool on his stepdad's table. We were still trying to jump on a bill at Lounge Ax in Chicago with Jawbreaker and Screeching Weasel, but the chances seemed less and less likely. So we wound up leaving for St. Louis, where we were supposed to open for Seven Year Bitch. With a night off between destinations, we decided to blow our $20 earnings from Blondie's on a cheap motel in southern Indiana.

As Scott was paying for a single-bed room for the six of us, a pack of pit bulls jumped from a station wagon and rampaged the parking lot like overgrown land-piranhas. One came running towards me and I jumped in the van, locking the door. Those nice Avail dogs taught me nothing.

Inside the motel room, the TV was busted, tile was missing all over the bathroom, the hot water had a beige tint, and mysterious dog hair covered the bedspread. Chuck sat cross-legged in a corner of the floor reading *Helter Skelter* beneath a strong yellow light, looking a little psycho. Things were getting weird.

Scott took a shower first; when he was done, Chuck jumped in. Thirty seconds later, Chuck came out in a towel, dripping wet.

"Scott, what the hell is this?" Chuck said, pointing to his foot.

Trapped in Chuck's toe hair was a gooey white substance.

No, I thought. It *couldn't* be.

"Oh, dude," Scott said, "I'm so sorry. I thought I cleaned up."

Everybody started howling. I freaked. I ran outside screaming.

"If you're gonna jack off in the shower," Chuck yelled to Scott, *"have the decency to clean it for the next guy."*

Fucking hell.

The next morning I woke up queasy. My upper back was sore from sleeping on the floor. I had carpet marks on my cheek and forehead, bits of unvacuumed micro-trash and crumbs in my hair.

After hours of uneventful driving through the ever-bland Midwest — the geographical equivalent of boiled pork — we pulled into a club in a supposedly rough part of St. Louis, though it looked okay to me. The space had been rented for the night, and we had to carry all of our equipment down precarious catwalk stairs to the basement, where the bands were playing. It had an old SoHo art-house feel to it — a stark, concrete space with glaring lightbulbs hanging on long cords from the high ceiling.

Upstairs, we were treated to a buffet that came with Seven Year Bitch's contract. The members of Seven Year Bitch spoke to us with a vague condescension specific to bands "on the rise." A few months earlier, they were featured in *Rolling Stone* — a band member had died of a heroin overdose, garnering them lots of publicity — and they were among the Seattle "foxcore" bands that were supposed to lead the female grunge revolution. To prove their importance (I guess), Seven Year Bitch's tour manager kept dropping names of various Seattle neo-celebrity fuckwads to us, people in Pearl Jam and Alice In Chains and other crappy bands we never gave two shits about. I hate name-dropping.

We met the people putting on the show, a well-mannered couple named Bill and Eve, as well as the second band on the bill, Nuisance. I owned a couple of Nuisance 7-inches; they blended traditional rock styles — Rush here, Lynyrd Skynyrd there — into a gritty, Jawbreaker-ish punk framework. We took a liking to them, especially singer-guitarist Andy, as well as their little entourage, a nice Australian couple following the band around the United States.

While slopping down vegan lasagna and trading tour anecdotes, Seven Year Bitch's guitarist recounted a story about staying at the home of a woman while on tour in California. It seems she had a newborn baby and left the band alone in the house, telling them to help themselves to anything to eat while she stayed elsewhere with the child. The guitarist checked the kitchen for a snack, including the fridge.

"I pulled out a Ziploc bag from the freezer and couldn't figure out what was in it," she said. "It looked weird. It took us a while to realize it was afterbirth."

Everyone stopped eating.

"Hold on — you're telling me she froze her afterbirth?" I asked, lowering my plate of lasagna.

"Yeah," she said.

"What the hell for?"

She looked at me like I was the class dunce. "So she could eat it," she said. "It's kind of a common hippie thing. It's supposed to be high in protein."

High in protein!

For the rest of the night we argued the validity of this afterbirth business. I thought she was putting us on, but the more paranoid of us felt a secret covenant existed among all women: they eat their babies' afterbirth and don't tell the men.

"Get real," Eve said later. "I'm not eating any afterbirth. Gross."

Having put the issue of edible afterbirth behind us, we finally took the stage. We decided not to make a set list, which was a rarity for us. We could never remember what songs to play, so (like most bands) we had to write them down in order.

I expected the acoustics to be terrible because the concrete room had such high ceilings, but the sound was surprisingly rich. The audience reacted well to our songs. It's amazing to watch strangers getting into your music, though they don't know you, the songs you've written, or where you come from.

Nuisance was excellent. Andy reminded me of an American Shane MacGowan. The guitar sound through his Marshall amp was strong and biting, making me yearn once again for a Marshall.

Seven Year Bitch's set was interesting. Lead singer Selene slinked in a sultry manner over garden-variety, Melvins-ish grunge riffing. She caressed her shoulders, baited the audience with "come hither" eyes, swung her hips, mussed up her bleached hair — a punk burlesque of sorts, subversively twisting traditional feminine wiles. Very sexy.

Though more than 200 people showed up in the course of the evening, the cash total didn't meet Seven Year Bitch's guarantee, and after the show they started complaining. Bill patiently explained he did all he could to promote it — a tough gig, since it was a Wednesday night — but the money simply wasn't there.

"And what about the little bands?" their manager said. "You have to pay them, too."

The "little bands" being, of course, Spoke and Nuisance.

It was getting tense. Everybody in Seven Year Bitch was yelling at Bill, who siphoned out some pocket money to help meet the guarantee. Their manager kept pressing for more, saying he was "holding out," but it was obvious to me he wasn't. Bill finally gave them the last of his personal money and said:

"Here. That's all I have. Now go buy your heroin."

There was a second of shocked silence, a second for the potency of the remark to set in. Even Bill seemed surprised at his cynical, mocking reference to the band's dead ex-guitarist.

"*You fucker!*"

Selene lunged at him, and with that Seven Year Bitch went collectively apeshit. I thought they were going to tear his eyes out. Though I could understand their sensitivity, a comment like that is inevitable when an honest dude like Bill is pushed to the wall. Somehow they settled things, but it was a bad scene. I was glad to see that band leave.

"Guys, I'm really sorry," Bill said to me and Scott afterwards. "I have nothing for you. They took it all. I can maybe scrape up 30 bucks tomorrow."

"Don't worry about it, man," Scott said.

Bill took us to his apartment, where we feasted on garlic fried in olive oil over cheap pasta. We discussed our tattoos, the war in Bosnia, the winery where Andy worked, East Bay punk, architecture, Australia, cigarette taxes, everything. We went to sleep happy.

The next day, after taking pictures of Fluffy by the St. Louis Arch, we had to make decisions about the remainder of the tour. A tentative New Orleans show looked sketchy, and a show in Tennessee had been cancelled weeks ago, which meant we had a few days until our last show in Pensacola. Crump suggested we spend the time at his Mom's cabin in Alabama. It sounded like a good plan.

I got comfortable in the van for the long drive, sprawling out as best as I could on a blanket, leaning my head against Scott's amp. I hadn't shaved for the whole tour, so by now I had a full, unkempt beard, with rigid little hairs protruding from my face like an electrified hedgehog. Whenever I glanced at myself in a mirror in the previous weeks, I found that I looked rather bizarre with my new beard, like an anarchist Hassidic.

The stiff hairs of my beard made my chin itchy, so I had to scratch it for about five minutes before I cracked open a used book I had bought for 50 cents in Greensboro. It was called *Points of Rebellion*, written in 1969 by Supreme Court Justice William O. Douglas.

Within five pages of Douglas' text, I was hooked. Writing about the civil, political and cultural turmoil of the Vietnam era, Douglas explained:

> *The dissent we witness is a reaffirmation in the faith in man; it is protest against living under rules and prejudices and attitudes that produce the extremes of wealth and poverty and that make us dedicated to the destruction of people through arms, bombs and gases, and that prepare us to think alike and be submissive objects for the regime of the computer. The dissent we witness is a protest against the belittling of man, against his debasement, against a society that makes "lawful" the exploitation of humans.*

Jeez, I thought, we could sure use a smattering of that dissent today. The debasement, belittling and exploitation of human beings has diminished little since Douglas wrote of it. As for individuals becoming "submissive objects for the regime of the computer," it's as if the American public is presently lining up to enlist by the millions.

With my nose deeply planted in Douglas' book, the hours and miles rolled by. The more I read of it, the more inspired — and unsettled — I became. It made me confront how much I've denied the obvious needs of the world, how much I've tuned out my own conscience, how much I've chosen a life of relative convenience and selfishness as a subservient consumer instead of bothering to contribute my skills and energy to achieve something better. What happened to that thing I called integrity?

It got me thinking of Spoke. What we were doing suddenly seemed so futile, so ineffectual and self-indulgent. We were wasting electricity, gasoline, manpower, time and creative energy on some half-assed compulsion to make noise — an endeavor that isn't remotely useful, much less revolutionary. Maybe that drunk girl in Richmond was right: with our loud, dumb songs, we had fooled ourselves into thinking that, because we were in a band, because we had momentarily captured a few people's attention, we were doing something *significant*.

"Fuck this shit! I've had it!"

Everyone in the van looked back at me.

"All of this isn't making a goddamn bit of difference!" I said. "It's pure self-deception! We're expending our energy for shit! We could have so much impact on this world but we're wasting our time playing bullshit!"

"What are you talking about?" Crump said, a little startled.

"There is so much need for action *everywhere*, and all I'm worried about is getting the right guitar sound out of my amp! What the fuck is that?"

I realized I wasn't making much sense, that my cohorts hadn't asked to be bombarded with a mouthful of hot rhetoric at this moment, and that maybe I was just in a bad mood because I was cooped up in a smelly van with too many guys.

"Jon," Scott said, "chill out."

Chill out indeed. Seething, exasperated, and with little else to do, I stopped reading and put my Walkman headphones on. Operation Ivy's "Sound System" was playing. Jesse Michaels was singing about the uplifting power of music — how, in the matter of one second, a song can kick in, take effect and *save* the listener, how the sound can somehow turn everything around.

To resist despair, that second makes you see...
To resist despair, because you can't change everything...
To resist despair, in this world
Is what it is to be free.

For now — *just for now* — that was my answer.

Arriving in Alabama, we met Crump's brother late that evening at his Mom's and drove to the cabin, a sparse riverfront bungalow hidden in the woods and linked to the river by a long dock. Except for the heaving wind, the chirps of birds and the occasional speedboat, it was absolutely quiet day and night. The heat was heavy and still and thick, making everyone move slowly.

Alabama was pure relaxation for us all — except Scott. He seemed agitated throughout. It began while we were swimming in the river, when everyone but Scott climbed up on the pier to dry off. With a box of Cheez-Its on the dock and Scott treading water a few feet away, we started throwing handfuls of Cheez-Its at Scott's head.

He submerged and re-surfaced, and we pelted him again. This set him off and he started cussing, so we threw yet more Cheez-Its.

Climbing onto the dock, Scott was almost shaking with anger. We weren't exactly sure why he was so incensed, but we weren't looking forward to his coming wrath. Facing us on the pier, barely restraining his fury, he screamed:

"*I... am... not... a... FISH!*"

We busted out in hysterics, rolling on the dock. Scott marched off to the cabin, all huffy.

"Fuck you all!" he yelled back to us.

"Come back, fish!" Anthony replied.

Later that night, Scott, still mad about the Cheez-Its, was brushing his teeth before going to sleep.

"Wha—? WHAT THE HELL IS THIS?"

He had mistaken a tube of Bengay pain-relief cream for toothpaste. He was brushing his teeth with Bengay.

"Who did this to me? Which of you assholes put the Ben Gay there?" He would not accept that it was an accident.

He wanted to call a doctor. I told him he'd be fine. I did the same thing once, except with my girlfriend's tube of Vagicil. He agreed that was worse.

But he wasn't convinced. When he called the poison control center and explained what happened, the operators laughed. "How's it taste?" they asked. It's not toxic, evidently.

After two days of intensive riverside lounging, we left Alabama for the final date of the tour, a show at Sluggo's in Pensacola, less than three hours away. With the end of our travels in sight, it was a bitterweset drive. The atmosphere in the van was dense with quiet reflection and a shared longing for the trip to continue.

We were playing with Bentley Tock, a standard post-collegiate alternative band, the kind who'd throw a cover of Bad Brains' "Pay to Cum" after a Toad the Wet Sprocket soundalike to showcase their supposed eclecticism. Bentley Tock would have been harmless enough if not for their T-shirts: in detailed gray airbrush, all too realistically depicted was a huge dick and balls. No crotch area, no waist — just limp, hanging genitals magnified 4,000 times. We agreed it was the ugliest thing we'd ever seen.

Sluggo's had a lot of bathroom grafitti. Before our set, I spent almost half an hour in the men's room deciphering the shaky script of drunks, rebels and other poets of the moment. There was the pretentious, pseudo-intellectual horseshit found in club restrooms everywhere:

EXISTENTIALISM IS A CONTRACEPTIVE TO USE WHEN SOMEONE IS FUCKING WITH YOUR MIND.

THERE IS NO LOVE... JUST BLOOD.

THE END OF SOMETHING IS THE CULMINATION OF EVERYTHING.

And a few hostile reactions to it:

SLUGGO'S IS FULL OF TOO MANY ENGLISH MAJORS. FORGIVE THEM.

LEARN TO SPELL GODDAMN IT.

I found one pretty good message chain:

DEAD MEN DON'T RAPE.

→ MEN WHO RAPE SHOULD DIE.

→ SO SHOULD ALL THE HYPOCRITES.

→ GET LAID BOB MASON.

Plus some near-brilliant quotes of limited, if any, implication:

NICK, WE'LL SUCK THE FRESCA OUT OF YOUR ASS ANY TIME.

BEER IS YOUR FRIEND.

JESSUP, WALK WITH ME. JESSUP, TALK WITH ME. JESSUP, KISS ME ON THE JAW.

AM I THE ONLY MAN WHO CAN FUCK HIMSELF IN THE ASS?

LSD SAVED MY LIFE.

YOUR MOMMA'S A HAMSTER.

THE REASON WE CUT OFF RACHEL'S HEAD WAS CUZ WE COULDN'T FIND JOHN BURT'S ASS.

ARE THE BLONDES HAPPENING?

And the most genius entry, written clearly and without explanation:

BOWEL FEAST.

In the dressing-room attic, Chuck found an inflatable sex doll which he named "Inga" and hid in his bass drum. It's not a real tour unless you bring home an inflatable sex doll.

On stage, after almost four weeks of performing, our instrumentation was as close to flawless as possible. For this show, we played each song with maximum precision, emotion and efficiency — no mistakes, no wasted energy. It was as if the instruments themselves were transparent and the songs came directly from the source of their creation. For us, it produced the sense of freedom and ecstacy we were always striving for. Whether the small audience at Sluggo's appreciated it or not, it was Spoke at full force.

Before crashing at our friend Jessie's house, we made one last trip to Waffle House. It was almost dawn and, like a dumbass, I ordered chili and a cheeseburger. I could feel the pangs in my stomach even before the first bite, while a very drunk Chuck was berating me for not wanting to play our next show in Gainesville naked.

"Chuck, if you get naked you're sitting behind a drum kit," I said. "Nobody will see you. If I get naked, I'm standing up front in everybody's face. Nobody wants to see that and I don't want to do it."

"You're getting conservative," he said. "You're turning into a conservative asshole."

"Well, you're turning into an asshole right now!"

"I think we should all get naked," he said, sulking over pancakes.

Jessie's roommates were awake when we returned at daybreak, and one of them started a groggy fight. They didn't want us sleeping there; they claimed too many bands had stayed over the past few months. Jessie said tough shit, they're here and they have no place else to go. Knowing we weren't wanted, we sheepishly looked for places to sleep in the house while the fighting continued, hoping they'd resolve it by the time we fell asleep. Scott, Anthony and Ethan spread out on the floor, Chuck and Crump found a bed to sprawl on, and I curled my body into a little ball on an ottoman. A few hours later, my throbbing back reminded me I had just slept on a goddamn ottoman.

We left Jessie and her cranky roommates at noon for Tommy's studio in Tallahassee. It was so hot it seemed even our cars were sweating, too hot for me to sleep for the drive, the kind of heat that makes you nauseous just to think.

My mind went foggy the second we pulled into Tallahassee. It was as if the Tallahassee air was replaced with pot smoke and the water with tequila, as if somebody gave me a lobotomy as we entered the city limits. Hours would pass in a haze; days would string along in bleary-eyed fluidity. Maybe all that sleeping in the van finally caught up with me.

We unloaded at Tommy's house. He was as accommodating as ever, slow to realize the hell we were about to drag him through: the 16-hour days of mixing down the same songs in his bedroom; the near-constant, high-frequency din of my amps, punctuated by my screaming vocals; our dirty clothes littered all over his living room. We would invade his home and take over his life for four days. As he confided to me later, we would push him "to the edge" — something I never wanted to do to Tommy Hamilton.

During our stay, I ended the tour diary with notes scribbled all over two pages, the kind of scrawled, paranoid rantings one might expect to fill the notebook of a mad scientist:

We're driving Tommy insane... everything sounds like hell... my amp's got hornets in it I swear... pizza in this town sucks... lost voice during 'Spank Your Inner Child'... beard's getting uglier, expect to find twigs in it... Chuck wants to do weird stoner song with laugh track or something and he thinks it's gonna sound like Unrest or Mercury Rev and it's the worst idea in the world, it's gonna ruin the whole record*... been constipated since we started recording... took bike ride and fell, rashed up left knee... listening to first Ride record, Drive Like Jehu, Minutemen, Government Issue for inspiration, ain't helping... ate a pear, haven't eaten a pear in years... can't time half the intros right... cat hair everywhere... Chuck's inflatable doll from Sluggo's is following me I swear... spilled sesame oil all over Tommy's counter...

With my vocal tracks finished and my libido nearly dead from neglect, I eventually found a moment of privacy in a shower to do the one thing I was agonizing to do for the last 27 days. My "campaign of constructive restraint" had finally come to an anticlimactic end. Conclusion: it ain't worth it.

When we left Tallahassee, we had a master recording of our new album. Having listened to it a hundred times in a hundred variations, we found it impossible to say if it was any good or not. We only knew that we were sick to death of hearing our own songs.

It took five hours to get home. I could hardly wait to get back to Gainesville. I missed the ordinary, obvious things most. The Spanish moss hanging from trees all over town. The "Kesl Special" breakfast at Coney Island Restaurant. The shadowy Student Ghetto streets. The dense, stifling humidity. The Duck Pond. The hot provolone-and-tomato sandwiches at Bagelville. The overgrown tropical greenery everywhere. The warm rain. The Hardback. The suiza sauce on the enchiladas at El Indio. The lazy pace. The crazy people. In such a short time, I never thought I would've missed this town so much.

---

* It didn't. It actually came out sounding pretty good.

After dropping off our equipment at the warehouse, the first order of business was to develope the pictures of Fluffy. They were like a photo documentary of the tour. Fluffy in ghetto Atlanta by the Somber Reptile. Fluffy at the Washington Monument. Fluffy on the New Jersey Turnpike after ditching the folks at the Temple of the Raging Chicken. Fluffy by the St. Louis Arch with Nuisance and their Australian entourage. Fluffy everywhere.

Early the next morning, before Ethan returned the van to his parents, we made a stop in the suburbs, gently placing Fluffy in the spot from which Scott swiped it four weeks before. Our tour masoct was back to lawn-gnome status.

We placed an envelope with the photos in the mailbox, along with a note Scott wrote in Fluffy's name, explaining (in part): *"I had to be emancipated, to leave my stationery place on the lawn to see the world!"* We drove off waving goodbye, knowing we'd never learn of the owners' reaction to their statue's mysterious reappearance.

We'd like to think Fluffy had a good time.

japan

To begin a new chapter you must close the old one.

FORTUNE COOKIE MAXIM

Scott gets bad insomnia. Compounding everyday stress with his midnight fears — fear of death, of loneliness, of aliens putting him in a space zoo — his mind blossoms darkly in those hours best spent asleep. Most people who know Scott and his smart-ass disposition rarely see that the core of his character is acutely sensitive. With nothing to distance himself from his worries and concerns, the desolation of evenings could haunt him terribly.

Of all his sleepless nights, none was more tortured than when he applied for a teaching position in Japan a few months before graduating. With three semesters of intensive Japanese language studies under his belt, he interviewed at the Japanese embassy in Miami. Among other questions, he was asked to explain the Japanese parliamentary system of government; to converse with the interviewer in German (which Scott studied in high school); to tell them (in Japanese) why he should get the job; and — no shit — to "define" Buddhism. He did.

After all of this, he was told he made the second string of applicants, which meant he would get the job in Japan only if a first-string applicant cancelled.

"What kind of bullshit is that?" I said to Scott. "What reputable organization would put a person's life on hold like that? And who the hell's more qualified than you?"

Needless to say, this put the band in limbo too.

So until the final decision came, Scott, not knowing on which side of the planet he'd be spending the next couple of years, went night after night without sleep.

"It's getting to the point I can't tell if I'm asleep or awake anymore," he told me.

After coming home from tour, the letter finally arrived — the one that would ultimately say *konnichiwa* or *sayonara* to two years abroad. Scott was all nerves — no surprise — and couldn't open it.

He had to smoke a cigarette, ripple his forehead a lot and sweat first.

"Open it!" I said.

He blew a final puff of smoke and threw his cigarette aside.

"All right," he said.

Standing on the SpokeHouse porch steps, he tore open the envelope slowly and removed the letter. He hesitated, then unfolded it.

He smiled. And as he continued reading, his smile grew wider.

I knew he'd get the job.

It was time to end our band.

noise

Music is natural law as related to the sense of hearing.

ANTON VON WEBERN

Okay. You're almost done reading. I now ask of you a humble task.

Find a pot. A large, metal one — a Dutch roaster-type pot, if you have it.

Now find a metal spoon, the biggest one you've got.

Take a seat.

Hold the pot upside-down on your lap, clutching its side with one hand. With your other hand, raise the spoon above your head and — without smacking yourself — strike the bottom of the pot as hard as you can, like a drum.

Do it.

Do it again.

Harder.

Again.

Try hitting twice a second.

Are your eyes blinking involuntarily? Is your heart racing? Do you find the noise distressing? Is a headache coming on? Or, in the midst of all this clamor, do you find something strangely fulfilling, maybe some wild release, some primal sense of satisfaction, despite the fact your neighbors are calling the cops?

It comes down to this:

Either you'll keep banging that pot or you won't.

If you do, you're a lot like us.

Start a band.

end here

We fluorish only for a moment.

HOMER

July 3, 1993, 2:27 a.m.

"Okay, all right, look everybody, I gotta tell y'all something that — *cut that shit out!*... C'mon, I'm being serious..."

Poor Scott. Here he was trying to convey his most sincere sentiments during our very last gig, and our so-called friends — most of them drunk, inattentive and stoked out of their minds — were pelting us with Tootsie Rolls (we had thrown a bagful from the stage) and yelling: "*Scott! Show us your butt!*"

"What you've done for us is — *shut the fuck up!* — er, I mean... we're really grateful that we've... uh... had all these friends to..."

It was no use.

"Fuck it," he said to me, dodging Tootsie Rolls. "Play the next goddamn song."

Almost 400 people packed into the back room of the Hardback to celebrate our last night as a band — and no joke, this was it. No reunions to embarass ourselves. No detritus of past glories. Our time was up, and a new generation of Gainesville bands was about to come forth and carry the torch further. We were determined to snuff out Spoke while we still had the chance.

This was also Paste Eater's last show, and they played a fine set immediately before us, complete with a cover of Big Black's "Deep Six." Since Ajo, Bombshell, Less Than Jake and Dig Doug played before them, we didn't hit the stage until around 2 a.m.

As our set began, Chuck took his seat behind the drums. He was dressed in a tuxedo. After each song, he'd shed an article of clothing until, finally, he was naked. "I need my third drumstick," he informed the (thoroughly disgusted) crowd.

Scott was putting on different suits between songs. At one point I turned around and saw him wearing what appeared to be some sort of astronaut suit, which I guess he thought was cool. What quite a few people did want to see was Scott naked, but he wouldn't oblige.

I manned the artillery. Besides the bag of Tootsie Rolls, I tossed out "Spoke cards" (National Hockey League trading cards with our name scrawled on them); pasta; female clothing (having been accused of sexism at previous shows for tossing out male clothing); an old vacuum cleaner; jellybeans; bondage magazines from Orlando; the collection of pennies I accumulated over the last year, probably close to $40; SpokeHouse garbage; and the entire contents of a large bag of white flour, which, when thrown on a row of sweaty people, makes a deceivingly thick "body paste." I also offered $10 (with bill in hand) for the underwear of SpokeHouse maniac Dave Frank, and it looked as if we were about to witness a panty-lynching, but Dave got away.

Naturally, we sounded awful — sloppy, off-time, out of tune, amps cutting in and out, the works. But with everyone bumping into us, stepping on us, throwing firecrackers at us, and falling ass-first into the mike stands, there was no hope. On the eve of our termination, we would suck because everybody was having too good of a time. We were not complaining.

Having blasted through 17 songs in an hour, my head was a mess. It seemed I was running on 33 r.p.m. as the rest of the world spun at 45. The entire room lunged, pogoed and flailed while I tried to keep balance with the microphone at my lips.

Within what seemed like minutes, an entire hour had passed and our set was almost completed. We could prolong the night only so long before we were a song away from concluding our existence as a band.

The final number, "Muse," was the only recorded song we did not release. We couldn't capture its live intensity at Tommy's studio, and trashing it seemed a better idea than documenting a lackluster version. This would be the last time anyone heard it, including us.

"Muse" began with a simple three-chord guitar hook, which I would play on the top pair of strings — the E and A — in rapid-fire, double-time succession. My lower palm would mute the strings, causing a restrained, tense tone. The bass and drums were silent.

After a full minute of this repetition, I'd start singing the opening lyrics over the guitar line. My voice and the over-modulated buzz of the strings echoed through the Hardback's high-ceilinged chamber, and as I shut my eyes, it sounded like my guitar and I were in the room alone. My throat was hurting, buckling — that tight, familiar ache before sobbing. Scott and Chuck, who didn't sing this part but knew the words, joined in.

This is how this song was meant to be heard, I thought. Taut. Hushed. Intense.

With my eyes still closed, a recurring vision came forth, one that often emerged during this song: a spark slowly burning down a long fuse to an explosive at the end. Even audience members who didn't know "Muse" could probably sense its impending detonation.

By the time the long, constrained preface ran its course, we could do nothing to keep it from igniting. At precisely the correct moment — a moment determined less by tempo than feel — we cracked "Muse" open.

Drums slammed in. Bass shook the room. The muted guitar gave way to a savage roar.

My spine clenched and everything seemed to go white.

As I screamed the chorus, my body was channeled into the furious sawing motion of my strumming arm, my pick bashing back and forth against the strings hard and fast like a piston. My head was spinning; my flesh chilled. I couldn't tell what the audience was doing, what Scott and Chuck were doing, or if I was even there. Only this beautiful, unremitting noise seemed present and real.

This was it: a sonic explosion, an audio manifestation of fire unleashed.

This was why I wanted to make music.

Though we'd usually grind "Muse" to a screeching halt, pulling the reins on it suddenly and abruptly, we now chose to derail it, choking the song in angry feedback and dying wails.

I turned my amps to top volume. I grabbed my guitar by the neck, flung it over my head and smashed it on the stage floor. My amps bellowed as pick-ups, knobs and switches flew off the body with each blow. If this band wouldn't survive, neither would the guitar that helped spawn it.

I hammered and hammered, beating the guitar to oblivion, until only the carcass of a maple plank remained. My hands ached and my eyes burned as the guitar and I laid in pieces on the stage — ending the song, the show and the band.

Awash with spit, tears and sweat, I crawled into the crowd. The remaining audience — mostly friends who had seen us from the first show on — cheered, laughed, stared, heckled, cried. I looked back to see how my bandmates fared. Scott had jumped into his amp; Chuck had trashed his drums. Both were recovering.

Returning to the stage, I laid on my back, feverish and alone. Barely above the throbbing wail of my amps mourning the guitar I destroyed, I heard one last round of applause. And with that, our musical contribution — minuscule at best — was over.

We aspired to create melodious noise and wring every ounce of joy from it; we did. But of our duration together, nothing was more clear and absolute than this moment of undoing, this severance of ourselves from the voice we called Spoke. Saturated in heat, haze and noise, it felt, if only for a moment, as if we had been born into something better. As if we had become as pure and true as the sounds we tried to create. As if we had, without intent, laid waste to the whole motherfucking world.

It felt, in a sense, very much like perfection.

Gone.

No more.

Done.

thanks

This is living, not to live unto oneself.

MENANDER

Scott and Christie Adams, Adventures In Immortality, Ajo, Keith Allison, Bill Allred, Arcwelder, Jason Armadillo, Jen Ashley, Assuck, Avail, Frank Barber and Kaile Adney, Kathie and Bonnie Baker, Ed Ballinger, Barcelona House, Dave Bargeon, Oscar Beauchamp, Eric Blake, Anatol Blass, Jason Blomquist, Phil Blumell, Bombshell, Sean Bonner and Caryn Coleman, Doug Boone, Erik Botsford, Bryan Bowers, Heather Brockway, Randy Brownell, Bill Bryson, Kurt Burja, Burrito Brothers, Alan and Tina Bushnell, Jay Buzella and Lonnie, Chris and Todd Campisi, Erik Carlson, Casey Carnathan, Fred Carter, Jen Carter, Drew Cateraul, Kathy Chilimagras, Clairmel, Cleo the cat, Mike Clifton, Bill Clower, Mitch Collins, Aaron Cometbus, John Cook, Andy Costello, Brian Costello, Katey and Mike Costello, John Cotter and Julie Esbjorn, Brian Cotter, Crain, Crazy Greg, Crisis Under Control, Bill Crump, Danarchy, Rob Dark, Sven Davies, Mike Davis, Phyllis Dawson, Dave Decker, Scott Dempsey, Denature, Patty and Luis Diaz, Mike DiGiovanni, Christine Djuric, Brian and Jim Doherty, Lali Donovan, Don's Ex-Girlfriend, Don't Be One, Jason Dooley, Trey Dukes, Ethan Duran, Erikh Ebejer, Mark Ehret, Meredith Ellis, Mike Elverado, Jim Faherty, Fluffy Kitty, 411, Gabe Fowler, Dave Frank and Joanna Mickey, Travis Fristoe, Frolic, Fugazi, Tim Furnish, Jennifer Fusco, Ryan Gallagher, Matt Geiger, Jon Glass, Lynora Goode, Shannon Gordon, Jack Graham, Ben Gray, Sean Gregorczyk, Margaret Griffis, John Grigsby, Grinch, Gruel, Tommy Hamilton, Hardback Cafe, Matt Harmon, Mike Headbone (dec.), Helmet, Steve Heritage, Holger Herrmann, Dan Higgins, Brian Hoben, Jeff Horne, Hot Water Music (Jason Black, George Rebello, Chuck Regan, Chris Wollard), Kerri Howell, Heather Howes, Henry de la Hoz, Andy Huegel, Richard Huegel (dec.), Eric Hulce (dec.), Patrick Hughes, Robin Hunicke, Hyde & Zeke's Records Crew (Chaz, Bill, Mike), Rachel Ibarra,

Craig Ingerto, Matt Jackson, Lauren Jagnow and Nick St. Angelo, Major Jarman, Jawbox (Bill Barbot, Zach Barocas, Kim Coletta, J Robbins, Adam Wade), The Jeffersons, Renee Jessup, Jay Johnson, Liz Johnson, Brian Jones, Sam Jones, Jorge in Miami, Andy Jung, Randi Kaufmann, Jen Kapioski, Christie Kennamer and P.J., Kigo the cat, Steve Kosiba, Ava Lassiter, Sean Latrelle, Richie Lalwler, Jay Laws, Lazy Susan, Less Than Jake (Vinnie Sciorelli, Chris DeMakes, Roger Twig, Buddy Schaub), Michelle Levine, Nancy Lincoln, Jeff London, Karl Lueders, Phil Lynott (dec.), Ian MacKaye, C.C. MacLimon, Kevin Manning, Jim and Jon Marburger, Jen Mass, *Maximum Rock'n'Roll*, Elizabeth McGovern, Rob McGregor, Curt Meissner, the Melon Twins, Erika Merchant, Dave Milenski, Jessica Mills, Laura Minor, Julie Montgomery, Chris Montross, *Moon Magazine*, Jen Moore, Kristy Moss, Meghan Mull, Naiomi's Hair, Bob Nana and Friction, Craig Nelson, Noi, Tom Nordlie, Nuisance, Dan O'Mahoney, Eileen O'Neill and Jason, Orlando crew, Greg Orloff, Ivan Osorio, Ovum Posse (Joyce, Karen, Heather), Pat Pagano, Tim Pagonas & Lisa, Paste Eater, Kalpesh Patel and Katherine, Tracy Penza, Marcy Petersen, Guy Picciotto, Chris Pierce, Mark Piotrowski, Jessica Polito, Rob Ponzio, Vanessa Porter, Potential Frenzy, Alyse Preston and Jacob Ware, Gail & Jim Preston, Quicksand, Radon, Rob Ray, Jo Raye, Red Riders, Sarah Reeser, Rein Sanction, John Reis, Mike Rennie, Ann Resh, Lewis Resh (dec.), Vince and Cheryl Resh, Wyatt Roberts, Rodan, Liz Rogers, Miles Roguish, Trey Romano, Kevin Rose and Heather MacInenny, Howie Rosenfeld, Tamara Sabine, Derek St. Pierre, George Sanders, Greg & Mark Saracino, Linda Saracino, Sylvia Saracino, Sarasota/Bradenton crew, Viv Savage, Anthony Sciletti, Schoolkids Records crew (Whitey, Raymond, Nikki), Shudder To Think, Scott Sinclair, Stephanie Sinclair, Don Sizemore, Slap Of Reality, Derek Smalls, Clay Smith, Jack and Chris Spattafora, Sprocket the cat (dec.), Cathy St. Denis, David St. Hubbins, Steve Sostak, Victoria Stagg, Scott Stanner, Wade Starrett, Ben Stillwell, Shawn Strange, Stretch Armstrong, Jen Sunderland and Roy, Surgery, Matt Sweeting, Mike Taylor, Var Thelin, Tone Unknown, Nigel Tufnel, Angie and Jen Tyre, Alex Ulloa, Tom Walls, Steve-O Ware, Weakling, Bill Weisner, Brent Wilson, Leigh Withers, Corey Witt, Wordsworth, Jim Wysolmierski, Joe Voisin, Ken Volkmann, Jessie Willis, Mike "Woogie" Wogemuth, John Yates, Brian Yeager, Yesterday & Today Records, The Youngies, Brett Zeeb, Mike Zuber and anybody who actually paid to see us.

Viva pastacore.

VIPER PRESS PRESENTS: "BLUE FIRE HEREAFTER"

160-PAGE BOOKZINE BY JON RESH

**PUNK
ART
SCIENCE
HISTORY
DEATH
SEX
FOOD
DEVIANCE
LOVE
LANGUAGE
AND EVERYTHING
ELSE THAT
MAKES LIFE
WORTH LIVING**

PLUS:
SNAZZY GRAPHICS
THAT DON'T
HURT YOUR EYES.
BOOK-BOUND
FULL-COLOR COVER.
AND NO DAMN ADS.

INCLUDES INTERVIEWS, ESSAYS,
COMMENTARY & COMICS ABOUT

- *D. BOON*
- *APOCALYPSE SCENARIOS*
- *PI*
- *PHOTOGRAPHER
  GLEN E. FRIEDMAN*
- *VOLTAIRE*
- *FRIES*
- *VIRGIL FINLAY*
- *LASER INVENTOR
  CHARLES TOWNES*
- *SLEEP DEPRIVATION*
- *ROACHES*
- *PURE CAP*
- *CHICAGO CUBS
  ORGANIST GARY PRESSEY*
- *GUILLOTINES*
- *INVESTIGATIVE SOCIAL
  WORKER GEORGE SANDERS*
- *JAYWALKING*

AND MORE UNHINGED DRIVEL

"I could probably name 2.3 million bands whose music has made some impact on my life, but when it comes to zines there are only about a handful. This is one of them, and it sits at the top."

ZEEN

"Quite possibly the best one-man effort I've seen in five years. Graphically kick ass and inspiring."

FLIPSIDE

"With so many zines watering down their overall quality, Viper Press Presents is striking because of its quality, front-to-back."

NEW CITY

"An incredible project. The layout and design is superb."

DEAL WITH IT

"Very comparable to The Baffler — but way more rad."

ROCKTOBER

"What is admirable about Blue Fire Hereafter — besides the amazing move to reject all forms of advertising — is how it is classy and well-made while simulaneously keeping the solipsistic attitude of being a zine."

BADABOOM GRAMAPHONE